PRO TACTICS™

TACKLE REPAIR & MAINTENANCE

PRO TACTICS™ SERIES

PRO TACTICS™

TACKLE REPAIR & MAINTENANCE

Use the Secrets of the Pros to
Get the Most from Your Tackle

Kevin Dallmier

THE LYONS PRESS
Guilford, Connecticut
An imprint of The Globe Pequot Press

To buy books in quantity for corporate use
or incentives, call **(800) 962–0973**
or e-mail **premiums@GlobePequot.com**.

The Lyons Press is an imprint of The Globe Pequot Press.
Pro Tactics is a trademark of Morris Book Publishing, LLC.

All interior photos by Kevin Dallmier
Text design by Peter Holm (Sterling Hill Productions) and Libby Kingsbury

Library of Congress Cataloging-in-Publication Data

Dallmier, Kevin, 1968-
  Tackle repair & maintenance : use the secrets of the pros to get the
most from your tackle / Kevin Dallmier.
    p. cm.
  At head of title: Pro Tactics
  Includes index.
  ISBN 978-1-59921-417-7
  1. Fishing tackle—Maintenance and repair. I. Title. II. Title:
Tackle repair and maintenance. III. Title: Pro Tactics.
  SH447.D15 2009
  799.1028'4—dc22
                                                    2008028260
Printed in China
10 9 8 7 6 5 4 3 2 1

The author and The Globe Pequot Press assume no liability for accidents happening to, or injuries sustained by, readers who engage in the activities described in this book.

For Lisa and Kali at home,
and all of those with whom
I have enjoyed time on the water.

CONTENTS

■ Cody Marchant with Gulf of Mexico spadefish—Young anglers have little patience for gear that does not work properly. Maintain the gear, and many pleasant days on the water will follow.

Why Maintain Your Fishing Equipment?

In this day and age, the time-honored tradition of maintaining the old to avoid buying the new seems to have fallen out of favor. You only have to look around to see that the message being sent is to buy the latest, greatest thing; use it until it "wears out," which in many cases is synonymous with "needs maintenance"; and then throw it in the trash and go buy the next latest, greatest thing. While this approach may improve the bottom line of manufacturers and advertisers, all it does for the avid angler is deplete the kitty of fun money that could be used to take that long-awaited fishing trip to an exotic locale, upgrade to a bigger boat, or put to some other good use.

Beyond the simple dollars and cents approach, time is priceless, especially free time best spent on the water. A lost opportunity is just that—lost. You can never get it back, so make the most of it when it comes. Consider the following hypothetical situation:

As the five o'clock whistle blew, the angler hurriedly threw an outfit in the back of his pickup truck and headed for a favorite pond. Conditions were perfect, with overcast skies and just enough wind to put a ripple on the water. There was great anticipation of what the evening would bring.

The bite was on. For the first hour or so, the action was good. As darkness neared, it became phenomenal. The angler could barely contain his glee. Fishing this easy was a rare occurrence, if not a once-in-a-lifetime event. All the stars were in alignment this evening, and the fish gods were smiling.

After releasing yet another chunky bass, the angler noticed baitfish skipping from the water next to a submerged stump, then a huge swirl. A trophy fish had thrown caution to the wind and was using the twilight conditions as cover to move shallow to feed.

The setup was perfect. All the angler had to do was close in and make a good cast. The steps of the perfect presentation ran through the angler's mind: cast beyond the stump to keep from spooking the fish, retrieve the lure into the strike zone, and then wait to feel the strike before setting the hook on a fish of a lifetime. The angler picked out his target and fired off a perfect cast. Before the lure had even hit the water, he engaged the trusty old baitcasting reel that had served him well over so many years.

This time, though, things didn't go as usual. The buzzbait hit the water and began sinking to the bottom. The angler cranked ever more furiously on the reel, trying to bring the lure to the top where it could work its magic, but to no avail. Puzzled, the angler looked down, and then finally realized that although he was cranking, the spool wasn't turning. The angler could only watch as the trophy fish struck the surface a few more times before fading into the depths. The angler loaded up and headed home, cursing the bad luck and vowing this would never happen again.

▓ **When a big fish puts your tackle to the test, nothing beats the peace of mind of knowing it is up to the challenge.**

Does this story in any way sound familiar? Murphy's Law is well known, and anglers aren't immune. In fact, Murphy seems to take particular delight in playing his shenanigans on hapless anglers, in this case using a worn-out pinion gear as his plaything. With Murphy's help, it failed in the middle of fantastic fishing, which led to missing an almost sure thing on a huge fish and also the untimely end of a great trip. If the failing condition of that small but critical part had been detected during an annual checkup, it could have been easily replaced, stymieing Murphy's plans.

Basic reel maintenance is not that difficult, but it is very important. Quality fishing reels are manufactured to high standards, but that doesn't mean they are maintenance free. In fact, to get the best performance, the need for periodic maintenance is absolute. Fail to maintain the reel, and the premium price you paid for performance is all for naught. A dirty high-end reel won't work much better than a clean bargain-bin reel.

Performance isn't the only issue where cleaning and maintenance come into play. Life span is another. If you maintain a quality reel properly, there is no reason it shouldn't literally last a lifetime. You can expect to replace a few minor parts due to normal wear and tear along the way, but those instances will be few and far between.

To prove this point, the next time you spend a day on the water with an angler who has seen his share of sunrises and carefully maintains his equipment, take a close look at his tackle. Odds are you will see some reels that were rolling off the production line back when you were still trying to learn to drink from a straw. Just because they are old doesn't mean they aren't good. Take the original Zebco Cardinal spinning reels, for example. Long out of production, many are still going strong and command premium prices at flea markets and online auction sites. A reel that appreciates in value is the exception, of course, but it illustrates that in the long run it pays to buy quality and then maintain your investment.

The final thing to consider is the pride taken in a job well done. A lovingly maintained piece of fishing tackle is just more fun to use. It carries with it all the memories of big fish caught, and of the friends and family who were there to share the experience, and you know how it will perform in any situation because you know the details of its inner workings. Most importantly, you know and take pride in the fact that it will work because you have ensured that it will through careful maintenance and repair.

Money spent on a new reel won't buy total peace of mind. What you are paying for is the manufacturer's promise of that peace of mind, but it doesn't always come. Quality equipment should be backed up by a solid warranty, but warranties don't do you any good in the middle of a fishing trip. Peace of mind is a very rewarding thing, and the hours spent achieving it are

Salt water is very corrosive and is hard on fishing tackle. The rough green areas on this reel are places where corrosion has begun to pit the metal parts. Corrosion that has advanced this far is difficult to remove, though there are some products on the market that will dissolve it away.

fine sediment is mixed in with the water, and when that material is carried into a reel's moving parts along with the water, it is the equivalent of dropping a pinch of fine sand into the reel. Combined with grease and oil, the grit becomes almost a cutting agent and goes to work wearing down moving parts.

The same goes for salt, which is incredibly corrosive. Without plenty of tender loving care, cheap equipment won't stand up to saltwater use at all. Even quality reels need much more care if regularly used in salt water compared to fresh water.

This brings us to the key point of maintaining your fishing tackle and the purpose of this book, and that is proper maintenance. Maintenance can be broken down into three basic types.

The first type we will call *breakdown maintenance*. This approach can be described as waiting until equipment fails to repair or replace it. It is the approach many anglers follow but is one to avoid. Murphy's Law afflicts anglers like no others, and if something can go wrong at the worst time, it probably will. Think about it—if the only time you pay attention to your equipment is when it fails you, how do you think it will treat you?

▌ The rough white coating on areas of this reel are salt deposits that must be thoroughly cleaned to prevent further corrosion and damage.

The second type, and the type of maintenance discussed in this book, is *preventive maintenance*. As the name implies, the idea is to prevent problems before they occur by periodically inspecting, servicing, cleaning, and/or replacing parts. This approach can be summarized as "you take care of it, it will take care of you."

The third type of maintenance is sort of an extension of preventive maintenance and is called *corrective maintenance*. This is described as improving equipment components so preventive maintenance can be carried out more reliably. For example, say you have a fishing reel with chrome bearings that are forever rusting and freezing up. Those bearings can be upgraded to the more corrosion-resistant stainless steel or even a ceramic material, thus heading off a problem that even normal preventive maintenance wasn't able to solve.

There isn't a best "one size fits all" approach to preventive maintenance. Each piece of equipment is different. The key to success is to develop a logical and effective system and then *follow the system*.

For complicated pieces of tackle like reels, frequent basic maintenance along with a fixed-interval component replacement and overhaul schedule is an excellent approach. For the most simple tackle—a fish hook, for example—testing the hook for sharpness and inspecting it for rust before you tie it on would be all that is required. Other tackle, like rods and waders, will fall somewhere in between.

No system is worth having unless you follow it. Although at first it may seem like too much trouble, after a short period of keeping maintenance first and foremost in your mind, it will become second nature and just another part of pursuing your hobby.

CHAPTER TWO

Basic Tools and Supplies

As with any task, having the right tools for the job is very important. Fortunately, the tools and supplies needed for tackle maintenance are not extensive, and you likely already have many in your tool drawer at home. Although basic household tools will suffice for tasks like tightening up a loose screw on a landing net frame, if you are going to maintain reels, there are some special tools that will make the job much easier.

The most important tool in your reel maintenance box is a quality set of precision screwdrivers in both regular and Phillips head. A set that includes Phillips #00, #0, and #1, and regular sizes 1.5 mm, 2 mm,

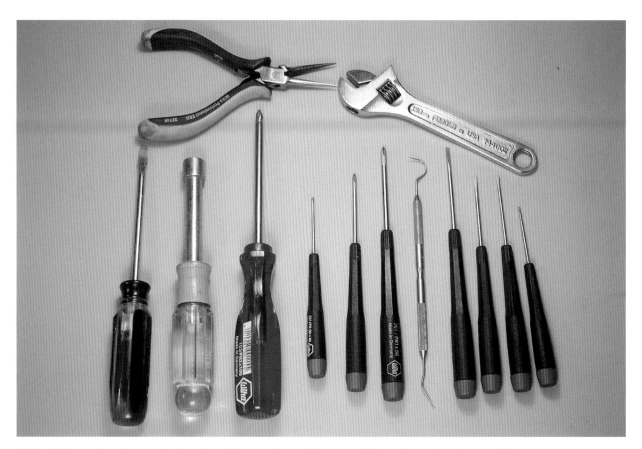

▋ Tools for reel repair are simple. A quality set of precision screwdrivers in various sizes, miniature pliers, a probe, and a few other common hand tools are all you need.

2.5 mm, and 3 mm, along with a standard-size $^3/_{16}$-inch regular and #2 Phillips, will cover nearly all the bases. The key here is to buy quality and to always use the right size for the job. Quality screwdrivers will stand up to much more use and abuse without the edges bending or rounding off. Using the wrong-size screwdriver or one with rounded edges on a screw is sure to lead to disaster, including stripping or rounding off the screw head or the screwdriver sliding off the screw and damaging a nearby part. A quality set of screwdrivers will be your best friend at the reel bench, so don't shortchange yourself—buy quality.

Along with your screwdriver set should be a set of precision needle-nose pliers, a set of regular slip-joint pliers, a small adjustable wrench, and some sort of probe useful for finagling small parts into place. A dental pick works great for this task. If you plan on servicing baitcasters, you might want to consider obtaining a 10 mm nut driver. The handle nut on nearly all baitcasters is this size, and the nut driver is best suited for the task of removing or tightening it, although an adjustable wrench will get the job done too. Avoid the temptation of using pliers for this or similar tasks. Pliers will suffice in a pinch for tightening or removing nuts, but are not meant for this application and will eventually lead to a scarred or rounded-off nut, not to mention a set of scraped knuckles.

Along with the hand tools, all that is required are a few Q-tips, old toothbrushes, clean rags, and some small containers to hold parts during disassembly and cleaning. Q-tips are great for getting into small places to clean and also for applying a light film of oil. Old toothbrushes are just right for cleaning reels, rod guides, etc. They are big enough to cover some ground, but small enough to fit into confined spaces. Also, the nylon bristles are stiff enough to remove all but the most stubborn dirt, but won't harm or scratch delicate parts. One trick for cleaning the tiniest of crevices or cleaning the inside of a hole, say on a pinion gear, is to visit your local pharmacy and pick up one of the very small brushes designed to clean orthodontic work and braces. These brushes have bristles attached to a flexible wire shaft and can fit into nearly any space. Rags are useful for wiping down large parts and also keeping your hands clean of excess grease and oil. Small containers will keep tiny parts from getting up and walking off, as they are prone to do, and can also be used to soak parts in cleaning agents.

A household cleaner like Simple Green is a good choice for an all-around cleaning agent and degreaser. Mix according to the label, let the parts soak for a while, then go to work with an old toothbrush and Q-tips. Most reel repair shops use an industrial ultrasonic cleaner, basically a larger, more powerful version of jewelry cleaners available at discount stores. The ultrasonic cleaner speeds up the process and cuts down on the amount of hand

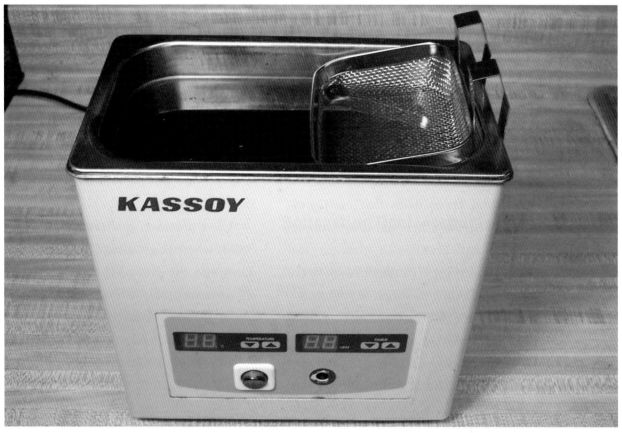

Ultrasonic cleaners do a great job of removing dirt and grime. Most reel repair shops use larger industrial models such as this one, but small ultrasonic cleaners marketed for home use will suffice.

brushing required. Perfectly acceptable results are possible with just some determination and elbow grease, though. Jewelry cleaners are a good compromise for those who do enough reels that they tire of the hand method, but not enough to justify investing in an industrial-strength unit.

A note about cleaning chemicals: Simple Green is biodegradable, proven to be safe, and will not harm any of the parts. Other seemingly very similar products may not be safe for all finishes. I learned this lesson the hard way. Luckily the damage was purely cosmetic and even more fortunately was on one of my personal

reels, not a customer's favorite baitcaster. If you wish to try a different product, do a test run first on a small, inconspicuous area to be sure it is safe for the material you are cleaning.

Although Simple Green is great on general dirt and grime and is a fair degreaser, for extremely greasy metal parts, mineral spirits or brake cleaner is the ticket. Both are good because they dry without leaving an oily film. A solvent like WD-40 will clean the parts, but it leaves behind an oily film that prevents the new grease and reel oil from sticking to the parts. Stubborn grease can be loosened by soaking the parts for a few minutes in line carriage to move back and forth across the spool as the handle is turned, resulting in the line being evenly distributed onto the spool. Some reels feature a disengaging level-wind that does not move or floats free when the reel is cast, while on other reels the level-wind moves back and forth on the cast.

Since the spool is spinning while the line is coming off it, care must be taken that the spool doesn't "overrun," i.e., feed off line faster than the lure being cast can pull it away from the reel. If this happens, the dreaded "backlash" occurs and the reel becomes a tangled mess. Many manufacturers have attempted to produce

a backlash-proof baitcasting reel, but so far technology has not been able to fully replace the "educated thumb" of a skilled angler.

Successfully casting a baitcasting reel means learning to control the spool by ever so lightly applying pressure with the thumb during the cast. Too much pressure and the cast will be short; too little pressure and a backlash can occur. All baitcasting reels have at least one if not several cast-control systems to help out, but some thumbing is still required.

The first system is adjusted through the cast-control cap on the side of the reel. Tightening the cap causes greater friction

▥ Some baitcasting reels are equipped with a set plate, which holds the gears and other parts. The set plate also commonly includes the brake drum, as seen here. The part protruding from the middle of the brake drum is the base of the pinion gear. Note the slot in the pinion gear that mates up with the spool when the reel is engaged.

between the ends of the spool axle and the cast-control shims that the tips of the axle spin on. The greater the tension, the more friction the spool must overcome to spin.

The second system is the tried-and-true centrifugal brake system. It works by two or more brake blocks sliding on small pins attached to the spool. The side of the spool equipped with the brake blocks is recessed into a brake drum that is part of the reel's frame, side plate, or if so equipped, a piece called the set plate that fits into the side of the frame and serves as a mounting point for the drive shaft, gears, anti-reverse dog, and linkage mechanisms. As the spool accelerates on the cast, centrifugal force slides the brake blocks outward on the pins, where they make contact with the brake drum and slow the spool down because of increased friction, i.e., the brake blocks rubbing against the brake drum. As the spool slows, there is less centrifugal force to move the blocks out and braking decreases. The system works well but is not consistent throughout the cast since spool revolution speed varies from start to finish, requiring a little work with the thumb to prevent a backlash. However, the advantage to this is that longer casts are possible since equal braking force is not being applied the whole time, as is the case on the first and third systems.

■ On this reel, the brake drum is found in the side plate on the side opposite the reel handle. In the middle of the assembly is one of the bearings that supports the spool shaft. Look very closely on the spool to see the small, narrow brake blocks that are extended by centrifugal force during the cast.

The third system that was quite popular for some time is a magnetic cast-control system. Designs vary, but the idea is to use magnetic force to cause more or less resistance to spool rotation to prevent an overrun. Magnetic systems tend to be of most use at the beginning of the cast but become a detriment to casting distance by the end because the magnetic resistance is constant throughout, whether it is truly needed or not.

On a reel equipped with all three systems, it is quite possible to adjust the settings to where a backlash-free cast can be made without ever thumbing the spool. However, casting distance and accuracy will suffer greatly, which defeats the purpose of using a baitcasting reel to begin with. In the hands of an experienced caster, baitcasting reels are amazingly accurate. You can literally drop a lure in a coffee cup from 50 feet away. But to achieve these feats of casting prowess, the cast-control systems have to be backed off enough to leave most of the control of the reel up to the caster's deft touch, not simple mechanical force.

The baitcasting reel's design is relatively simple to understand. The handle is attached to a driveshaft, and on the driveshaft is a main gear. As the main gear turns on the retrieve, it meshes with a smaller pinion gear. The size and tooth count of these gears is what dictates the reel's gear ratio. When the reel is engaged, a slot on the end of the pinion gear is seated against a squared-off portion of the spool axle (or in reels that don't have a fixed axle spool, a piece on the spool itself). Power goes from the handle to the main gear to the pinion gear to the spool.

A drag system allows line to be pulled off the reel even when it is engaged, say when a big fish is hooked and must be given some line to prevent the line from breaking. The drag system works through friction. One or more drag washers sit on top of the main gear with a metal plate or plates pressing down, sandwiching the drag washers between them. As the drag star is tightened, the drag washers are sandwiched tighter, and more force is required to overcome the friction and let the main gear spin backward on the shaft, allowing line to come off the spool. On the retrieve, friction from the drag is the only thing holding the reel "in gear" to where the spool will turn and line will be taken up.

To illustrate the basics of how a drag system works, pick up a baitcasting reel and back the drag star completely out. Now turn the reel. Very possibly the handle will turn but the spool won't, or hardly at all. Now tighten the drag star a turn or two. The spool will now likely spin when the handle is turned. But, put your thumb on the spool while turning the handle and see what happens. The handle keeps turning but the spool stops with only light pressure. Tighten up the drag a few more turns and repeat. You can still stop the spool with your thumb, but it takes more force to keep the handle turning because of the increased friction on the drag plates

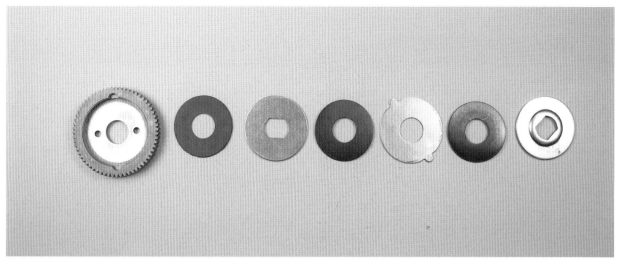

■ A main gear and drag washer set. The drag washers and plate sit inside the cupped portion of the gear. As the drag star is tightened, more tension is put on the drag stack and the increased friction tightens the drag.

and washers. If you keep repeating the process on a reel with a strong drag, you will get to the point where you can't turn the crank with the spool held immobile by the thumb—the friction is just too great to overcome.

As an aside, a good way to test drag is to pull line off the reel or the equivalent, hold the spool immobile with the thumb, and turn the handle. Either way, the drag should "slip" smoothly and steadily, not herky-jerky. A drag that stutters and jerks is a surefire means of losing the fish of a lifetime when the line breaks or the hook pulls loose. A smooth drag skillfully applied will whip a fish weighing many times the line's breaking strength.

As we have read, the handle spins the driveshaft that spins the gears that spin the spool, so how does the level-wind—or line carriage, as it is sometimes called—move back and forth to distribute the line? Things get a little complicated here. Each

reel make and model may have a slightly different method of moving the level-wind. However, all include the basics of a worm shaft, or worm gear, which is a grooved shaft running the width of the reel. The level-wind pawl is held inside the line carriage by a threaded nut cap. The pawl is crescent-shaped on one end, and this crescent runs inside the track, or grooves, on the worm shaft. Spinning the worm shaft causes the pawl to follow the track, bringing the line carriage along with it.

The basic power to complete this action is, of course, supplied by turning the handle, but how the energy gets to the worm gear is a little more complicated and can involve some parts called *idle gears*. On some reels, there are no idle gears; instead, a toothed gear on the end of the worm shaft mates with the main gear. On other reels, a separate gear is situated under the main gear on the driveshaft, and it is this gear that mates with the worm shaft gear. On

■ On this design a small gear on the end of the worm shaft mates directly with the main gear to rotate the worm shaft as the driveshaft turns to move the line carriage back and forth to evenly distribute line on the spool.

still other designs, the route is even more circuitous. The idle gear may be located in the side plate of the reel on the opposite side of the handle. The main gear turns the pinion gear to turn the spool. On the other end of the spool is a small gear that mates with an idle gear that matches up to the toothed gear on the worm shaft. This probably sounds more complicated than it is. A minute or two studying the reel with the side plates removed so you can see the reel's inner workings will make it all clear.

This is all important to understand because idle gears are a common source of failure. They are usually plastic or nylon, not brass or some other metal. This is by

design. The nylon gear serves as a built-in weak point. If excessive force is applied to the reel's drive train, the nylon idle gear will strip against the pressure of the metal gears, preventing damage to other gears and components. On reels that have seen a lot of use, the teeth of the idle gear may begin to wear away from meshing with the metal gear teeth, causing the reel to feel rough on the retrieve. Idle gears are inexpensive, and it would be a good idea to keep one on hand along with other commonly replaced parts.

Another system that is useful to understand is how the reel disengages so the spool can spin freely for the cast. For this

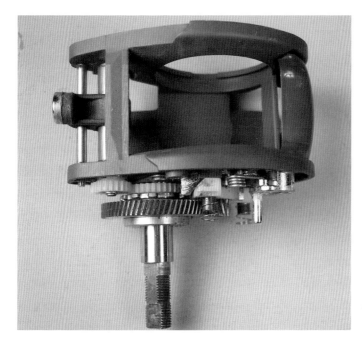

This design uses a gear at the base of the driveshaft to turn another smaller gear on the worm shaft to rotate the worm shaft as the driveshaft turns to move the line carriage back and forth to evenly distribute line on the spool.

This design uses an idle gear on the side opposite the handle to move the line carriage back and forth across the reel. The spool is also equipped with a gear, and as the spool turns, that gear turns the gear seen here, which mates up with a gear on the end of the worm shaft. Look closely at this gear to see the damaged gear teeth, a common problem.

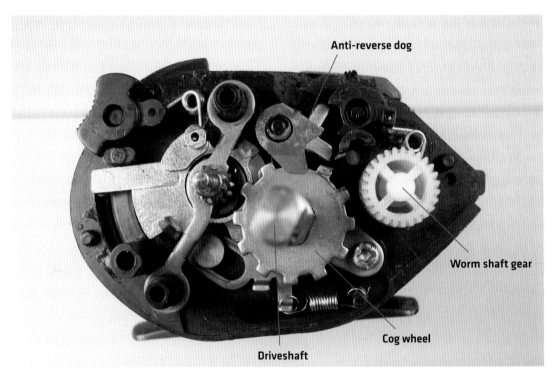

Anti-reverse dog

Worm shaft gear

Cog wheel

Driveshaft

▓ Note the anti-reverse dog-and-cog wheel at the top center of the photo. As the driveshaft turns clockwise on the retrieve, the dog lifts up and out of the way. When the driveshaft moves backward, the dog drops down to engage the cog wheel and prevent the reel from turning in reverse.

▓ The anti-reverse dog-and-cog wheel in the locked position.

▓ The anti-reverse dog-and-cog wheel in the unlocked position.

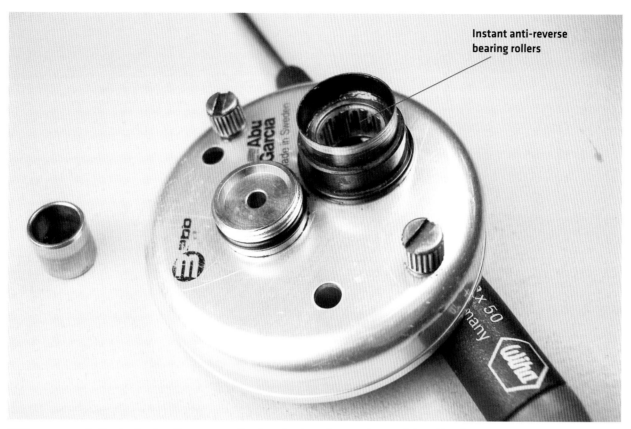

Instant anti-reverse bearing rollers

On some reels the instant anti-reverse roller bearing is an integral part of the side plate. Note the rollers inside the cage and the fingerlike projections that allow the rollers to turn forward but lock the reel as soon as the driveshaft and roller-bearing sleeve begin to turn backward.

that is the same shape as the case, so the bearing assembly is held immobile. On some reels the roller bearing is actually an integral part of the side plate itself.

Each slot in the cage that holds a roller is equipped with some sort of spring device, usually a springy plastic finger that is part of the cage. As the reel is cranked forward, the sleeve spins freely with the rollers inside the cage. But as soon as the sleeve stops spinning or begins to move ever so slightly in the reverse direction, the springs push the rollers into a locked position, grabbing hold of the sleeve and preventing it—and thus the driveshaft and handle—from turning backward. Now, the

drag regulates how line control comes off the reel since the driveshaft cannot turn backward. This happens so quickly that in terms of a fishing application, it seems "instant." There is no play or slop in the system if it is working correctly.

About the only drawback to instant anti-reverse is that the system is sensitive to lubrication and dirt. Too much or the wrong type of lubrication prevents the rollers from moving into position to get a good "hold" on the sleeve when it begins to turn backward, resulting in slippage. Too much dirt and grime working its way into the bearing case can cause the same problem by gumming up the delicate springs and rollers. Finally, since the parts are located in the side plate instead of farther into the reel, water and dirt are able to find their way into the instant anti-reverse roller-bearing case and cannot easily be rinsed out without disassembling the reel. Especially in salt water, rust and corrosion will quickly start to develop. In the event this happens, the best-case scenario is the reel becomes a little rough and the instant anti-reverse begins to work intermittently. A minor case of this can usually be resolved through cleaning. The worst-case scenario is the anti-reverse sleeve actually corrodes to the rollers and the reel is frozen—the handle will not turn in either direction.

This requires replacing both the instant anti-reverse roller bearing, which is one of the more expensive parts on a baitcasting reel, and the instant anti-reverse sleeve.

Basic Maintenance

Now that we understand a little about how a baitcasting reel works, let's consider the steps for a basic lubrication that should be performed every few trips in fresh water and more often in salt water. Basic lubrication can be completed in just a few minutes and does not require completely breaking down the reel.

■ Most baitcasting reels have a spool with a fixed axle. However, some reels have the ultracast design where the axle is not fixed and the spool spins freely on the axle, not with the axle. In the middle of the spool is a spool bearing, and the brake blocks are also visible.

To start with, wipe the reel down with a damp cloth, or if used in salt water, rinse the reel by gently spraying it with fresh water and then wipe dry. Take off the handle retainer nut cover or the handle nut itself. If you see a hole in the end of the driveshaft (not all reels are designed this way), place a drop of oil on the end of the driveshaft where it spins on the support shaft that protrudes from the set plate. Next, place one drop of oil at each end of the handle knobs. Take off the cast-control cap, place one drop of oil inside, and replace the cap. Next, turn the reel over and place one drop of oil on each end of the worm gear and one in the middle. Finally, remove the pawl cap and place one drop of oil at the base of the pawl. On many reels, the pawl cap does not need to be removed to perform this task since the cap has a hole in it just for this purpose.

For those mechanically inclined, you can take the basic lubrication process a little further by removing the left side plate. Some reels have a quick-release feature, while others may require loosening the thumbscrews on the handle side plate to release the opposite side plate from the reel. Refer to your owner's manual for hints on how to remove the side plate.

Once the side plate is removed, take out the spool and set it aside. Place one drop of oil on the shim located underneath the side plate bearing or bushing. On a reel equipped with centrifugal brakes (most are), swab the brake drum with a clean Q-tip to remove any dirt or foreign matter that will slow down the brake blocks as they rub against the drum during the cast. Once clean, swab the drum with a Q-tip very lightly moistened with reel oil, then follow up with a clean Q-tip. The idea is to leave just a microscopic film of oil on the brake drum. Too much oil will cause inconsistent braking and reduce casting distance.

Next, pick up the spool and clean the spool shaft, including the ends, with a clean cloth or Q-tip followed by a swab with a Q-tip lightly moistened with oil. If there is a bearing fixed to the spool shaft, lube it with one drop of oil. When handling the spool, be very careful not to drop it. Dropping can bend the spool axle, which will cause serious problems or even require the replacement of the spool with a new one. Spools are one of the more expensive reel parts, so handle with care! Slide all brake blocks to the center position so they will fit back into the brake drum without being pinched. Insert the spool back in the reel frame. Keep in mind that the squared-off part of the spool axle must mate up with the slotted end of the pinion gear. Getting the two to mate the first time can be tricky, so use patience and don't force the process. Reattach the side plate.

To finish the process, lightly coat the reel with silicone spray and wipe with a clean, lint-free cloth. Cover the reel to protect it from dust during storage, and it will be ready for your next trip.

it engages the spool. If you found what looked like brass shavings in the area of the pinion gear when you took the reel apart, you definitely have a problem. Shavings or not, if the pinion gear slot is gouged and the sides or corners are rounded off, think about replacing the gear. This problem is greatly exacerbated by anglers who have a habit of engaging the reel while the spool is still spinning at the end of the cast. The brass pinion gear is softer than the spool axle. If the reel is engaged while the spool is still spinning, as the squared axle mates with the pinion slot, the spinning spool axle starts to wear away the slot in the brass pinion gear.

Also closely examine the line guide carriage to make sure there is no grooving. Over time the constant friction from the line rubbing across these parts will begin to cut a groove and abrade your line. Braided line will hasten this problem, but even soft monofilament can do it in time. Fail to replace this part, and the result can be a lost fish as the line rubs up against the rough spot on the line guide and gets cut!

The final parts to examine are the shims in the cast-control cap and the left side plate. If a shim is just slightly dimpled, simply flip it over if you don't have any new ones available. For shims in worse condition, replace them. Shims are very cheap parts, and a heavily dimpled shim will cut down on casting distance. The very tips of the spool axle ride on the shims, and a heavily dimpled shim allows more surface contact between the tip of the spool axle and the shim, resulting in greater friction and a subsequent decline in casting distance.

Now it is time to start reassembling the reel. But first, a word about lubrication.

■ On the left is a worn pawl that needs to be replaced. Note the score marks and how the pawl is partially worn away. By comparison, on the right is a pawl with a little corrosion but no serious damage.

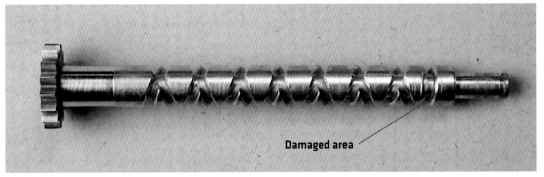

Damaged area

■ A worm shaft that has been damaged by a bad level-wind pawl. Note the scoring in the grooves, and on the extreme right, gouged areas and places the chroming has been worn away.

Where does the grease go, and where does the oil go? In general, grease the gears and pivot points, and oil the bearings and bushings. In other words, grease parts that work at low speed under heavy load, and oil parts that work at high speed under light loads. Also, a note on drag washers. Some reels have a "dry drag" and some a "wet drag." Do not grease dry drags. Wet drags should be very lightly greased with special drag grease. Check with your manufacturer if you are not sure which system your reel uses.

Reassemble the reel in the reverse order of how you took it apart. Have your schematic with the notes and the digital pictures handy to serve as a guide. It is also a good idea to group the parts in some logical order on your workbench before you begin. Doing so will help you avoid forgetting about a small part until you complete the process only to find there are parts left over. Nothing is more frustrating than having to undo everything you just did to get back far enough into the reel to install the overlooked part.

Once everything is complete, test the reel. Tie on a practice plug and make a few casts. Does the reel cast and retrieve smoothly? Does the reel clutch fully disengage to make a cast, then crisply engage when you turn the handle? Does the cast control have a good range of adjustment? Play with the drag. Does it release line smoothly and under a range of loads? If all of these conditions are met, you have a reel that is as good as or better than the day you purchased it and ready to faithfully serve you for another season.

Corrective Maintenance

Baitcasting reels offer a lot of potential for corrective maintenance. If you are the tinkerer type and aren't satisfied until you have coaxed the last bit of performance out of your equipment, there are some things you can do to trick out your baitcasting reels.

The easiest task to perform is to upgrade the bearings. Bearings are rated by the Annular Bearing Engineering Council (ABEC) of the American Bearing Manufacturers Association. The higher the rating, the tighter the tolerances of the bearing and theoretically the better the bearing should perform. Bearings are rated on the ABEC system of 1 through 9, with 9 having the tightest tolerances. Replacing a reel's stock bearings with ABEC 5 or ABEC 7 bearings is a popular upgrade. The bearings to consider upgrading are the ones that support the spool. These bearings are usually located in the reel's side plates, or in the spool itself on some reels.

With the exception of some vintage models, fishing reel bearings are metric. The bearing size is expressed as "inside diameter × outside diameter × width," for example, 3 × 10 × 4. A set of calipers will tell you the size of the bearings you need to order. Some aftermarket suppliers catering to the fishing reel market have charts available that list the bearings found in popular reel models. Although bearings often come prelubricated, it is a good idea to flush the bearings and relube them with one drop of your favorite lightweight reel oil to achieve the best performance.

The bearings found in most quality fishing reels are stainless steel. However, full ceramic and ceramic hybrid (ceramic balls, stainless case) are also available and may be a good idea if you fish in salt water or want to buy the absolute best bearings on the market.

Some high-quality reels feature ball bearings to support the worm shaft instead of the traditional bushings. It may be possible to upgrade your current reel to one with this feature. The same holds true for gear retrieve ratios. A reel with a fast ratio can sometimes be dropped to a slower ratio, and vice versa, by replacing the existing gears with a main gear and pinion gear from a similar model.

Some baitcasters come with a bait clicker, or line-out alarm, feature. This allows the reel to be left disengaged, and an alarm sounds when line is pulled off the reel by a fish taking the bait and running with it. It too can sometimes be added to a reel that doesn't already have the feature.

The key to the upgrades described above is that there has to be a very similar model by the same manufacturer that has the feature you desire. For example, the hugely popular green Shimano Curado series of reels was produced in three different gear retrieve ratios. The CU-200B had a 6.2:1 ratio, the CU-200B5 had a 5.0:1 ratio, and the CU-200B38 had a slow 3.8:1 ratio. These models were all identical except for the gear ratio. To convert a fast CU-200B to a slow CU-200B38, all that is needed is to acquire the gear set for the CU-200B38 and put those gears in the CU-200B. It's just a few minutes' work, and it's much cheaper than buying a completely different reel. Not all reels can be converted, however, or a reel may be able to be converted in one aspect but not another. Contact a fishing reel parts supplier to determine what is available for your model.

Drag washer upgrades are also possible. Aftermarket drag washers made of carbon fiber and other high-tech materials are available for many reels. Better drag washers result in smoother start-up and more consistency, with less "fade" on hard-running fish. Contact a reel parts supplier or search the Internet to find out what is available for your reel.

The last corrective maintenance to consider doesn't involve any new parts, just some time. Although the normal cleaning process will do wonders for your reel's performance, if you want to go all out, you can fine-tune the reel to eke out that last bit of performance.

Any time two parts rub against each other, friction occurs. When casting a baitcasting reel, the main friction points are where the spool shaft rubs against other parts. The increased friction shortens

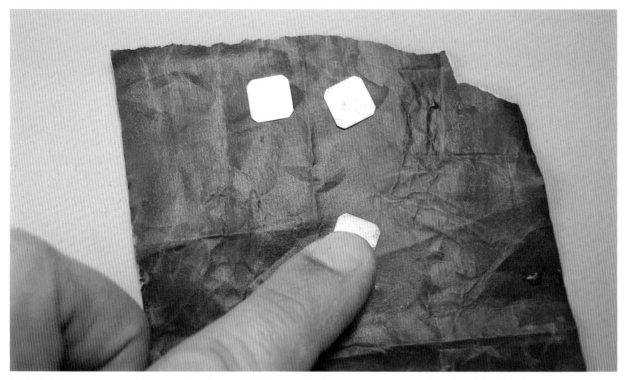

■ Polishing a cast-control shim that the end of the spool axle spins on. A smooth, mirrorlike finish will give the best performance. Note how the polished shim in the upper left is mirror bright and free of any tarnish compared to the unpolished shim on the right.

the cast length from what it could be and can also contribute to backlashes from inconsistent spool braking. If the friction between these parts can be reduced, better performance should follow. The way to reduce this friction is to fine-tune the parts by polishing the contact points. The smoother the finish on the parts, the less friction. Think of rubbing two pieces of patent leather against each other versus two pieces of suede leather. Which will rub against each other with the least resistance?

The areas that need to be polished are the brass cast-control shims, spool shaft ends (for fixed-axle spools), the inside of the pinion gear, and the brake drum. Begin by

cleaning the reel as usual, but before reassembling it, polish the parts listed above. Start by polishing with 600-grit wet-dry sandpaper, then 1,500 grit, then finish up with a liquid polish like Brasso. Between steps, clean the parts with alcohol or brake cleaner, and wipe to remove any residue. The key thing to remember during the process is that polishing does not mean grinding. The intent is not to grind away the material, just to polish what is there so the part remains the same size but has a mirrorlike finish. For example, don't go overboard and work the inside of the pinion gear to the point where there is more play between the pinion gear hole and the spool shaft than when you started. Just

■ This rotary tool equipped with a split toothpick and a narrow strip of very fine-grit sandpaper is useful for polishing inside tight places when fine-tuning a reel for maximum performance.

polish the inside of the hole—don't work it to the point where you have enlarged the hole.

The way to polish with a rotary tool is to take a round toothpick or very small-diameter dowel rod and cut a slit in the end with a razor knife, then cut a narrow strip of fine-grit sandpaper and place the end in the slit. Wrap the sandpaper around the wood shaft. The diameter is controlled by how long a strip of sandpaper is used. This nifty little tool will allow you to polish all shapes and in small recessed places, including holes. To finish up the process with the liquid polish, replace the sandpaper strip with a piece of cotton or use a Q-tip cut in half in the rotary tool. Apply the polish to the cotton and go to work.

Cast-control shims are easily polished. Just work them briskly back and forth across some wet sandpaper using your fingertip to achieve a shiny finish. Another method is to secure the shims on some double-sided sticky tape and polish using a rotary tool.

Due to their shape and location, the pinion gear and brake drum will need to be polished with a rotary tool. Polish the inside of the pinion gear hole until it gleams when you look through it. On the cast, the pinion gear is pulled away from the spool, but the spool shaft still spins inside the pinion gear, which is why it needs polished. Polish the brake drum by working the tool around the drum, never staying in one place. Polishing the brake drum will provide a smooth, even surface for the brake blocks to rub against.

Finally, polish the ends of the spool shaft. This is a little more difficult than the other parts. The easiest way is to chuck the spool into a drill, drill press, or lathe, but you must protect the spool shaft from being marred. One way is to wrap the shaft in several layers of tape and avoid overtightening the chuck. Carefully apply power to spin the spool and then use your fingers to gently apply the sandpaper to the other end of the shaft. Using just your fingers as backing, there is enough give in the sandpaper that it will follow the existing rounded shape of the end of the spool shaft. Do not polish the areas of the shaft that pass through the spool bearings, just the very ends and where the pinion gear rides on the shaft. The tolerances between the bearings and the shaft are very tight and should not be polished lest too much play be introduced between the inner bearing races and the shaft. Doing so will reduce the effectiveness of the bearings. Remember, spools are expensive, so treat them with care!

For many types of angling, baitcasters are the best tool for the job. Follow the steps in this chapter to get the most from these wonderful pieces of tackle.

■ A spinning reel with a cross-block oscillation design. As the main gear turns, the large teeth on the gear turn the pinion gear and spool. The smaller teeth turn the gear inside the housing under the main shaft. A stud on that gear moves within a groove on the cross block, which is secured to the main shaft by a screw or clip.

gear, or by a keyed shaft attached to the handle that slides through a keyed hole in the main gear. Not only does the main gear mesh with the pinion gear to turn the rotor, it also meshes with an oscillation gear. A stud on the oscillation gear slides inside an oscillating slider or a cross block (an alternate system seen on a few older reels has an arm from a stud on the main gear linked to the main shaft to oscillate the shaft and spool as the main gear turns).

The slider or block is fixed to the main shaft, and as the oscillation gear is turned, the stud moves inside the groove of the slider, causing the main shaft to move in

and out. Since the spool is attached to the main shaft, the spool also moves in and out, causing the line to be evenly wrapped onto the spool as the rotor spins.

The system described above is the most common method of oscillation. However, some high-end spinning reels have borrowed from baitcasting reel design, and instead of using an oscillation gear and slider, they use a worm gear and pawl design. Although more complicated, these reels tend to be very smooth on the retrieve. The basic idea is the same, but in this case the main gear turns the pinion gear, which mates up with a small

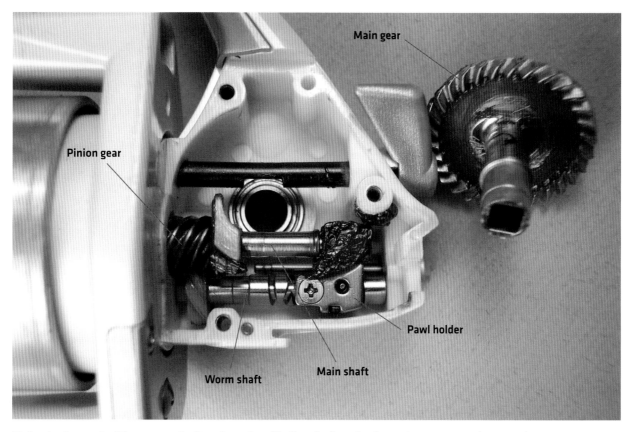

■ A spinning reel with a worm shaft and pawl oscillation design. As the main gear turns, it turns the pinion gear, which turns a small gear attached to the worm shaft. As the worm shaft turns, the pawl in the holder attached to the main shaft follows the track, moving the main shaft in and out to oscillate the spool.

gear on the end of the worm shaft. As the gear turns, it rotates the worm shaft. A small block holding a pawl is attached to the end of the main shaft. As the worm shaft turns, the pawl follows the grooves in the worm gear, causing the main shaft to move in and out, thereby oscillating the spool.

The drag system on a spinning reel works the same as any other drag system, relying on friction between plates and washers to get the job done. Anglers have two choices, front drags and rear drags, and which one is better is merely a point of personal preference.

Front drag systems have the drag washers and plates in the spool itself. A knob is turned to increase tension on the plates, preventing the spool from giving out line as easily. In this design, the spool can turn independently of the shaft it is mounted on.

On a rear drag reel, the washers, plates, and adjustment knob are at the rear of the reel. This drag does not act directly on the spool itself; instead, the drag acts on the main shaft, which the spool is fixed to. In other words, the design does not allow the spool to turn independently of the shaft. As the spool turns, playing out

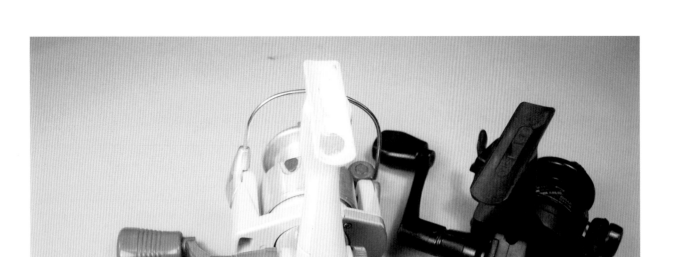

No drag knob   Drag knob

■ Two types of spinning reels. The reel on the left is a front drag reel, where the drag washers are contained in the spool itself and the drag is adjusted by a knob on the front of the spool. On the right is a rear drag reel, with the drag adjustment knob on the back. On this design the drag plates and washers are contained in the reel body.

line under a heavy load, the main shaft also turns.

Spinning reels differ from baitcasting reels in that nearly all come with a selector switch. This allows the angler to selectively switch between an anti-reverse system that directs control of line being pulled off the spool to the drag system, and a system that leaves how much (if any) line is played off the reel up to the angler, who turns the handle backward to give up line just as it is cranked forward to take in line. The latter is called *backreeling*, and many spinning reel anglers prefer to trust their backreeling ability over a mechanical drag system.

The two basic anti-reverse systems used in spinning reels are the anti-reverse dog system and, in more modern reels, the instant anti-reverse roller-bearing system. The mechanics of how these two systems work are discussed in detail in the baitcasting reel chapter. For the instant anti-reverse roller-bearing system, the principal is exactly the same. A one-way roller bearing is secured to the body of the reel, either by screws or by placing the bearing in a keyed cup in the reel's body so it cannot spin. A sleeve that is keyed to fit the pinion gear turns inside the roller bearing. The pinion gear and thus the rotor can spin forward but not backward.

A switch isolates this feature if the angler chooses to leave the reel in backreel mode. The same baitcaster drawbacks apply in spinning reels—the roller bearing is sensitive to too much lubrication, and grime and corrosion can be a problem, especially in saltwater applications.

The anti-reverse dog-and-cog-wheel system is still common in spinning reels. While the basic principal is the same as in a baitcaster, since there is a lot of variation on how the job is performed in spinning reels, it isn't practical to describe all the possible configurations here. The anti-reverse system will either be located under the rotor or in the reel housing, but beyond that, there are many different designs. However, a basic overview is that some reels use a variant of the friction-type activation common in baitcasting reels, while others use a spring-tension system where the tension is actually keeping the dog in contact with the anti-reverse cog. Most veteran anglers are probably familiar with the "click-click-click" sound made by spinning reels not equipped with "silent anti-reverse." The

Oscillation arm

Anti-reverse mechanism

■ A spinning reel with a linkage arm oscillation design. A linkage arm connects a stud on the main gear to the end of the main shaft. As the gear turns, the main shaft moves the spool in and out. In the lower middle is the anti-reverse dog. When the anti-reverse is turned on, a spring keeps tension between the dog and the anti-reverse teeth. With this type of design, when the system is on there is always contact between the two parts.

clicking noise is the dog, under tension from the spring, skipping over each tooth on the cog wheel as line is retrieved. The cog wheel teeth are shaped in a way that allows the dog to easily skip from tooth to tooth when the reel is being cranked forward, but catch and hold when the cog wheel begins to turn in reverse.

The introduction of reels equipped with silent anti-reverse signaled the transition from a straight spring tension anti-reverse dog, where the dog was constantly making contact with the cog wheel, to one where the dog is held away from the cog wheel when the reel is moving forward (therefore the "silent") but is brought into contact with the cog wheel by friction activation when the reel begins to move backward. Just like on a baitcasting reel, when parts are turning one way, friction between the related parts in the system holds the dog up and out of the way, and when the parts move the other way, the friction moves the dog into place. Depending on the reel, this system can be mechanically very simple or rather complex, with several moving parts all working together to get the job done.

The final systems on a spinning reel that should be understood are the bail cocking and tripping mechanisms. Compared to other reel systems, these are often very simple, but they are also the number one source of problems with spinning reels. Since the bail is what holds the line, it must be opened, or "cocked," to allow line off the spool, and it must be closed,

or "tripped," to catch the line and direct it onto the line roller for line to be wound back onto the spool. Along with this task, the bail must stay in a closed position under opposing force on the other end of the line, say when a fish is hooked. All of this is achieved through springs, although a few reels are beginning to come on the market that achieve the same results through a set of magnets. But, since the bail-spring system is still far and away the most common, we will limit our discussion to it.

When you cock the bail to make a cast, the resistance felt is from the bail spring. The bail spring (or *springs* on some models) is located on the side of the rotor where the bail attaches to the rotor. The springs can be L-shaped with a coil in the middle and two legs, or on many vintage reels, a larger coil spring roughly the size of a shirt button. On either of these types of springs, the very ends of the spring are usually bent at a 90-degree angle and fit into a small hole on the rotor and on the bail arm.

Most modern reels have replaced the springs just described with a coil spring and plunger arrangement. The spring looks very much like the kind found in ballpoint pens, and there is a plunger-like part with one end that fits inside the spring and the other having a stud that fits in a hole on the bail arm. The advantage of this design is, unlike the first two springs described, these springs rarely if ever break, and the same goes for the plunger. On the other hand, a reel equipped with an L-shaped or large coil spring directly connected to the rotor

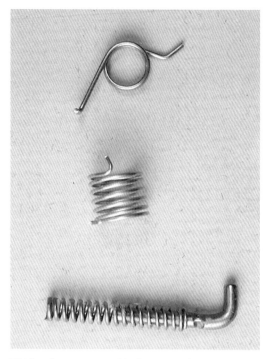

The three types of bail springs (top to bottom): L-shaped spring, coil spring, and spring and plunger design.

A spinning reel with an externally locking bail design in the bail-closed position.

and bail arm will eventually break or get too weak to do its job—it is only a matter of time. Most often, L-shaped springs break where one leg meets the coiled part in the middle of the spring. Large coil springs often break at a spot near where the end of the spring wire makes the 90-degree bend, or the bend itself will break. Since bail-spring breakage is such a common ailment, and there is little if any warning before it happens, it is always a good idea to carry a few spares in your field repair kit.

When the bail is cocked, it swings through an arc and is opened to the point where it "breaks over," or is in a fully open position. On some reels it is locked into the open position by a spring-loaded lever that slips into a slot on the end of the bail where it mounts to the rotor. When the

handle is turned after the cast, the rotor spins and the lever comes up against a trip mechanism that moves it back and out of the slot, allowing the bail spring to snap the bail shut. To overcome the resistance and move the lever to trip the bail, reels of this type must be turned smartly, and the result is a sharp jolt as everything snaps back into place. Another disadvantage is that once cocked open, the bail cannot be closed by hand, which, as we will discuss shortly, can be a detriment.

On the plus side, as long as everything is working properly, there is almost no chance for the bail to snap shut on its own during the cast. The bail snapping shut on the cast is of little consequence when casting a light crappie jig, but can be rather disconcerting when casting a heavy plug,

Once the task is completed, test the reel. Does it crank smoothly both forward and backward in backreel mode? Turn on the anti-reverse. Does it catch without hesitation? Does the bail cock smoothly and securely? Is the bail spring providing good resistance when cocking the bail? Does the bail snap closed with authority on the first rotation of the rotor when cranking the reel? Test the drag. Does it release line smoothly and under a range of loads? If all of these areas receive high marks, your reel is as good as new.

Corrective Maintenance

If you are the tinkerer type—and enjoy spinning reels but wish you could avoid the dreaded loops or bird's nest, where line comes off the spool in one big tangled and twisted mess—there may be some corrective maintenance you will want to consider.

Loops are caused by line twist. Using a poorly tuned lure that spins and twists your line is going to aggravate the problem, as is improperly spooling the reel with line (the coils of line should come off the feeder spool in the same direction they go on the reel spool). But, loops can and will happen, even when neither of these no-no's has taken place. Line twist and the associated loops are an inherent problem with how spinning reels function. The culprit is the bail wire. As the bail slaps against the slack line while turning when it

closes, twist is introduced to the line, and a loop is sure to follow sooner or later.

Some anglers try to avoid this problem by closing the bail manually at the end of the cast instead of turning the handle to activate the trip mechanism to snap the bail shut. But depending on the reel, this may not be an option. As you may recall from the discussion at the beginning of this chapter, on some reels the bail is locked open and cannot be closed by just bumping the bail wire over with your hand. The handle must be turned to spin the rotor to trip the bail. Also, the hand-closing method takes an extra bit of work with the off hand and also means you don't get as quick a grip back on the reel handle after the cast.

There is another option, however. It won't work on all reels, and it isn't for the faint of heart who are loathe to change anything about their favorite reel. This option is to perform corrective maintenance and custom modify your reel to do away with the bail entirely. Cut off the bail?! Isn't that an important part of my reel? The answer to that question is no, not really.

All that is needed to put line back on the spool is the bail arm and line roller—the rest of the bail wire is just something to catch the line and direct it to the roller after the cast, where it stays after that. Cut the bail wire off, and you will never have line twist or bird's nests again. So how does this work once the bail wire is gone?

To cast, you just lift the line off the roller with your index finger instead of holding

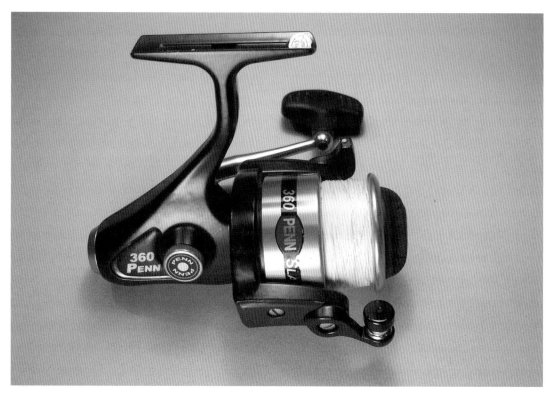

■ A spinning reel with the bail wire removed. This corrective maintenance action works on most reels, is easy to adapt to, and will virtually eliminate bird's nests and line twist.

the line with the finger and then cocking the bail open with your off hand. Make a normal cast. To begin the retrieve, you just use your finger to put the line back on the roller after the cast. Sounds difficult, you say? The best way to explain it is "pulling a trigger" with your finger while you turn the reel handle with your other hand. Your finger brings the line up closer to the rod, then the roller comes around and catches it and pulls it off your finger when you turn the handle. It takes a split second and is much easier and quicker than it sounds. Do it for ten minutes, and it will become second nature and you won't even have to think about it anymore. Believe it or not, the line won't fall off the roller, even when fishing a jig or some other lift-and-drop technique.

Before you take this step, though, there are a couple things to consider in determining if your reel is a good candidate. First, the modification works best on small- to medium-size reels. A larger reel is positioned too far away from the rod, and catching the line with your finger can be tough depending on the size of your hands. This can be easily determined, however. Just make a few casts, and at the end of each, instead of turning the handle to close the bail, try catching the line with your finger. If this works, it is time to move on to the next condition.

Most spinning reels have the bail spring on the bail arm side of the rotor, but not all. On some reels the spring is on the side opposite the bail arm, and these reels

■ Two conventional reels. The reel on the bottom is equipped with a level-wind and line carriage, while the reel on the top lacks this feature. Note the saltwater corrosion on the lower crossbar and reel foot on the top reel.

Basic Maintenance

Since conventional reels are so simple, there are not a lot of places on them that need to be lubricated. The handle knob, the spool shaft ends, and the drive-shaft pretty much cover the bases on most reels. Conventional reels are often equipped with lubrication ports in key places, which is a feature missing on most other types of reels. Lubrication ports utilize a small spring-loaded ball. The spring keeps the ball pushed outward to seal up the reel, but when the tip of an oiler is placed against the ball, the spring yields to let the ball move back and oil to flow into the port.

After every trip, wipe down the reel. If used in salt water, give the reel a thorough rinse with fresh water. Wipe the reel dry and lubricate it with a quality reel oil. Give the reel a coat of silicone spray for a protective finish, wipe with a clean cloth, and the reel is ready for storage.

Advanced Maintenance

For overhauling a conventional reel, since the same basic disassembly steps as those for a baitcasting reel are followed, disassembly and lubrication will not be discussed in detail here. Refer to the baitcasting reel chapter for a thorough discussion.

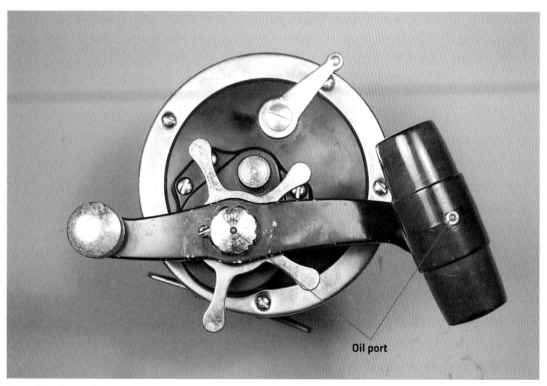

Oil port

■ A side view of a conventional reel. Note the oil ports in the center of the handle knob and the handle retainer screw. The small metal ball in the center is pressed out by a spring, sealing the opening. Oil is applied by pressing the ball inward with the tip of an oil applicator.

▦ **A fully disassembled conventional reel ready for service.**

▦ Conventional reels are often equipped with a bait clicker, or line-out alarm. A selector switch moves the click pawl into position to make contact with the large teeth visible on the end of the spool. Held onto the reel frame by a screw is the idle gear, part of the level-wind system.

If the drag plates are corroded, replace them. Drag washers should be pliable, not dried out and flaking away. If the drag washers do need to be replaced, now would be an excellent time to upgrade the reel by looking into some of the aftermarket high-tech drag washers that are available.

Inspect the gears for any signs of wear. Closely examine the other parts, and be sure to remove any corrosion or replace the part if necessary.

Now it is time to reassemble the reel. Since the basic process has already been described in the baitcasting reel chapter, we will limit our discussion to a specific

hurdle you are likely to encounter along the way: securing the bridge to the side plate while simultaneously installing the anti-reverse system. Depending on the reel, this task can be easy or it can be difficult, to say the least. Difficult does not mean impossible, though, and rest assured that each time you do it, the task will get easier. Although your reel may require a slightly different approach, the following is the basic process for reels equipped with an anti-reverse dog that is held in place by a side plate screw.

First, assemble the bridge parts by placing all the gears, drag washers, drag

■ A fully assembled bridge holding the main gear and the drag washers and plates. The bridge screws to the side plate that contains the pinion gear, pinion yoke and springs, and shift linkage.

plates, etc., on the bridge driveshaft. Next, with the side plate placed upside down on your workbench, install the pinion gear and pinion. Remember, the pinion springs go into the side plate and then the pinion yoke goes on top of them so the springs are sandwiched between the yoke and the side plate. Now, place the eccentric jack (the part that slides back and forth and moves the pinion yoke and gear away from the spool to disengage the reel) on the eccentric cam. This will help hold the pinion yoke in place for the rest of the process.

Refer to your notes for how the anti-reverse dog and spring are oriented to the side plate and bridge. Carefully pick up the side plate and hold it vertically, then pick up the bridge assembly and position it with the driveshaft through the hole in the side plate. Holding the plate vertically allows the bridge to be held so the drive-shaft is facing in a direction that will not allow the parts on it to slip off the shaft like they would if turned upside down. Position the bridge to where it is almost touching the side plate, but not quite. Slip the anti-reverse dog into place through the gap between the side plate and the bridge. The tip of the dog should be positioned between the base of the bridge and the underneath side of the main gear. Make sure the dog is oriented correctly—both to the cog wheel teeth and to itself (i.e., which side faces out or up).

Next, insert one side plate screw (remember from your notes that the smooth shaft screws go in the holes that match up with the pinion yoke springs) through the side plate hole and anti-reverse dog. Hold the screw in place to secure the anti-reverse dog—don't begin to thread it into the bridge. Now, insert another screw through the side plate hole opposite the anti-reverse. Thread the screw very slightly into the bridge to secure it, but not so far as to pull the bridge to the side plate, which would close the gap you are working in.

Your next step is to finagle the anti-reverse spring into place using a probe or miniature screwdriver. This task can be very tricky, like building a ship in a bottle, since you are working through a small gap while holding everything in place with your fingers. One technique that works well for small coil springs is to select a miniature Phillips screwdriver with a head just slightly larger than the inside diameter of the spring. Spread a little grease on the screwdriver head to help hold the spring, and stick the spring on the end of the screwdriver. Using the screwdriver, slide the spring through the gap until you feel the end of it catch in the squared-off part of the anti-reverse dog. Compress the spring slightly by pushing in with the screwdriver, then pinch with your fingers to close the gap between the bridge and side plate. While pinching the two parts together, slowly withdraw the screwdriver, and the end of the spring should slip into its place on the side plate. One way to think of it is that you are "scraping" the spring off the screwdriver.

While holding the bridge tight to the side plate with your fingers, turn the driveshaft forward then backward to make sure the anti-reverse is working. If so, congratulations—you have completed a difficult task. Keeping the bridge and side plate pinched tightly together, install the remaining side plate screws. Now that the side plate assembly is complete, you can finish reassembling the reel.

CHAPTER SIX

Spin-Casting Reel Maintenance and Repair

Spin-casting, or "closed-face," reels burst onto the scene shortly after World War II. They quickly caught on with anglers who loved the trouble-free and simple operation. The spin-casting reel is an attempt to solve the problem of backlash found in baitcasting reels, while also reducing the bird's nest and line loop problems inherent in spinning reels.

It would be safe to say that most American anglers cut their teeth on a spin-casting reel. The reel's simple and intuitive casting makes it a great choice for beginners. One could argue that the spinning reel is nearly as simple to learn and offers better performance, but there remains the problem of throwing loops or bird's nests.

Although spin-casters are often looked down upon as a novice's reel by experienced anglers, this is not entirely accurate. For many types of fishing, a quality spin-casting reel can do a perfectly fine job. Somewhat unfortunately, since spin-casting reels are marketed primarily to novice or casual anglers, they are often priced accordingly, and along with the low prices come poor-quality components and assembly. This results in anglers discounting all spin-casting reels as cheap and ineffective instead of being another tool at their disposal.

Spin-Casting Reel Mechanics

Like a spinning reel, spin-casters have a fixed spool. In addition, these reels have an external nose cone, or bell cover, that encloses and protects the fixed spool. There is a trade-off for this protection, though: The friction of the nose cone against the line as it comes off the spool slightly reduces casting distance compared to spinning reels.

The main difference in the design of spin-casting and spinning reels is how the line is wound back onto the spool. Spin-casters don't have the spinning reel's large bail wire and line roller. Instead, the "spinnerhead" is a metal cup with one or more line pickup pins. As the handle is turned, the spinnerhead turns with the pins extended to catch and hold the line and wind it onto the spool. With their fixed spool, spin-casting reels can cast lighter lures than baitcasting reels. One drawback

■ A spin-casting, or "closed-face," reel. These reels are very simple and easy to use, making them a good choice for beginners. They are low maintenance, too, since all the moving parts are enclosed and protected.

is that spin-casting reels have narrow spools with less line capacity than either a baitcasting or spinning reel.

To cast a closed-face reel, the angler simply depresses the button with his or her thumb and holds it in a depressed position until it is released at the proper time during the cast to send the lure on its way toward its intended target. This is how it works: When the thumb button is depressed, it pushes a shaft forward. The spinnerhead is attached to this shaft. As the spinnerhead moves forward, the spring-loaded line pickup pins retract into the spinnerhead, releasing the line. The

cup-shaped spinnerhead moves away from the fixed spool so the line can flow freely off the spool. To keep the lure from simply falling to the ground instead of being held near the rod tip for a cast, a rubber or nylon piece on the spinnerhead pinches the line against the inside of the bell cover, or a piece comes up to press the line against the lip of the spinnerhead. Either way, the line is held immobile, just like you would hold the line with your forefinger when using a spinning reel.

During the cast, the button can be depressed again to bring the lure to a sudden halt, or the line flowing out the end of

▧ **A spin-casting reel spinnerhead. Note the line pickup pin protruding from the spinnerhead. These are prone to wear and should be examined closely for grooves and rough areas that can damage the line.**

the bell cover can be feathered with finger pressure. At the end of the cast, turning the crank handle engages the reel by dropping the spinnerhead back over the spool, and the line pickup pins extend out automatically to catch the line and begin to wind it onto the spool. Like most other modern reels, spin-casters are equipped with some type of anti-reverse system and a drag system based on friction that plays out line in a controlled manner under a heavy load.

Although they are perfect for some applications, spin-casting reels in general are not well suited to large, powerful fish. The narrow spool limits line capacity, and the drag system often leaves much to be desired in terms of smoothness and range of adjustment. Spin-casting reels cannot match a quality spinning or baitcasting reel for smoothness on the retrieve, and the gear ratios are often relatively low, which is a drawback for some techniques. On the plus side, spin-casters are nearly foolproof and can take a lot of abuse before they fail. The reel's compact, enclosed design protects the inner workings from dirt and grime very well. Drop a baitcasting or spinning reel on a sandy shoreline, and you are asking for problems. Do the same to a spin-casting reel, and it likely will suffer no ill effects.

Basic Maintenance

Due to their foolproof design, spin-casting reels do not require frequent maintenance.

In fact, other than the handle knob, there are no lubrication points readily accessible without partially disassembling the reel. Fortunately, for just a basic service, disassembly is very simple.

First, remove the bell cover. Most thread off or are freed by a partial turn to release the bayonet-style mounts. Rinse the bell cover inside and out with soapy water. The bell cover tends to get rather dirty from grit and algae coming off the wet line as it feeds into the cover. If the bell cover is very dirty, casting distance will suffer since the line can't flow as freely through the cover. Also at this time, clean the spinnerhead of any buildup, especially around the pickup pins.

Next, examine the pickup pins on the spinnerhead to make sure no grooving has occurred from the friction of the line constantly moving across the same place on the pin. This is a common problem in spin-casting reels, and if it has occurred, order a new spinnerhead. (On some reels the pickup pins can be replaced independently without purchasing a complete spinnerhead assembly.) Failure to do this can result in the pickup pin nicking or abrading your line, resulting in a weak point.

On some reels removing the bell cover will allow the rear cover to come free, since the two parts thread together and hold each other to the reel body. In other cases the side plate can be taken off by removing a few screws, or if the rear housing is attached to the reel body by bayonet locks,

■ The internal workings of a typical spin-casting reel. These reels are very simple, consisting of a main gear, a pinion gear on a shaft that turns the spool, and a small anti-reverse dog that is hidden from sight behind the main gear.

the housing can be twisted a partial turn to release. Once this step is performed, the reel's inner workings should be easily accessible. Give the gears a little more grease if needed. Place a few drops of oil where the pinion gear shaft enters the reel body and where the main gear passes through the bushings or bearings on the reel body.

Reassemble the reel by installing the bell cover and rear cover or side plate. Wipe the exterior with a damp cloth, and the reel is ready for storage.

Advanced Maintenance

Periodic basic service will keep your spin-casting reel functioning in top form for quite some time. There is not a whole lot more to be gained by completely disassembling the reel, since most of the parts can be reached by removing the bell cover and rear cover or side plate. However, if your reel is having problems or seems in need of a more thorough cleaning and service, the process is generally the same as for basic maintenance, so we will only discuss a few key points along the way.

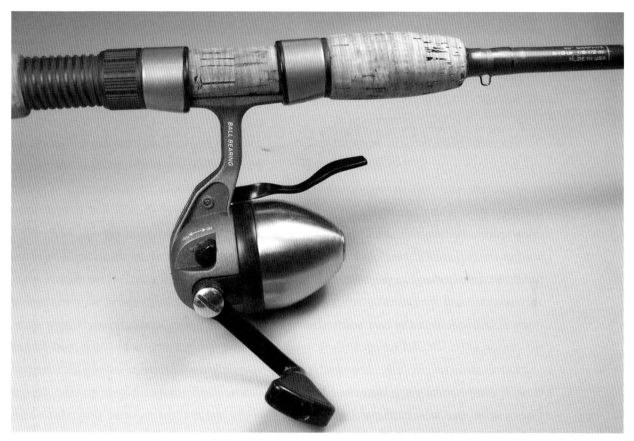

A variation of the basic spin-casting reel called an "underspin" reel. These reels have the same trouble-free operation but provide a more balanced feel by being positioned under the rod instead of on top of it.

After removing the bell cover, but before doing anything else, remove the spinnerhead. Some spinnerheads are held on the keyed shaft by a nut and are easily removed, while others screw onto the end of the threaded shaft. To remove the spinnerhead, hold the handle firmly in place with one hand and turn the spinnerhead in the same direction it spins when retrieving line. This should begin to thread the spinnerhead off the shaft.

Underneath the spinnerhead, the spool is likely held on by a large clip. Remove the clip and the spool, being sure to note the order of any drag plates, drag washers, or spacers. On many spin-casting reels, the drag system is associated with the spool, not the gears.

Now, begin to work on the rear of the reel. Remove the handle nut and handle. If any drag components are located under the handle, make note of them as you take them off.

The next step will vary depending on the reel and may take some deductive reasoning. The pinion gear shaft needs to come out from the back of the reel. On some reels it may simply slide out, while on others the main gear may be blocking the way, or there may even be some

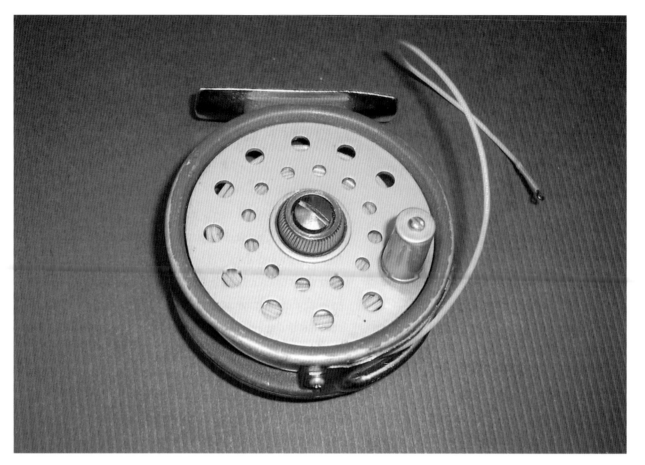

▉ **Assembled reel – A vintage single-action fly reel. These reels are very simple with only a few basic parts.**

which the palm of the hand is lightly held against the spinning spool, creating more drag as the fish takes line.

The next type of drag is a caliper system. As the drag is tightened, a caliper moves and pushes against the spool. The friction creates drag and slows the spinning spool.

The type of drag on most quality fly reels is a disc drag, which is very similar to the drags found in other types of reels. A large-diameter pad, or drag washer, is pushed against the spool's braking surface. The drag washer is often made of cork or can be some type of synthetic material like Teflon. Disc drags allow for fine adjustment and should provide smooth start-ups and consistent drag pressure.

Taking drag systems to new heights, the latest one uses an impeller immersed in a special multiviscosity fluid. With this type of drag, there is no adjustment needed based on the size of the fish. The system reacts to the speed at which line is being pulled off the spool by the fish. As the fish speeds up, the drag automatically increases.

■ Disassembled reel – The same vintage single-action fly reel reduced down to basic parts. The reel housing, the line spool, the drag washer and plate, and the retaining nut. Note the click pawl in the middle left of the housing. The pawl prevents the spool from spinning free and overrunning when line is being pulled off the reel.

Basic Maintenance

Fly reel maintenance is very easy. Periodically, rinse the reel in fresh water. This is especially important for reels used in salt water and must be done after every trip! The inner coils of fly line and backing can hold a lot of moisture and salt, so be sure to strip off enough line for the fresh water to flush away any deposits.

Remove the spool. The spool will probably have a threaded knob of some type holding it on, and perhaps a clip underneath the knob. Flush any exposed surfaces with copious amounts of warm, fresh water. Avoid the temptation to use high-pressure spray, though, since this could force sand and grit into areas where it doesn't need to be. Shake off the spool to remove excess water and let dry before reassembling.

Lightly grease the spindle the spool turns on. Place a drop of oil on any sealed spool bearing. If the reel is equipped with a one-way roller bearing, swab inside the bearing several times with a clean Q-tip to give the rod a more thorough cleaning by adding the following steps. Apply a coat of wax to the rod blank to restore its protective coating. If the rod is multipiece and has ferrules, lightly rub the male portion of the ferrule with some paraffin or wax to prevent it from sticking. To make cork grips look like new and improve their feel, take some very fine-grit waterproof sandpaper (available at auto parts stores), wet the rod grip, apply some hand soap to the sandpaper, and rub thoroughly. Rinse with fresh water and let dry.

Guide rings deserve special attention throughout the year. Inspect them for damage by slipping a Q-tip or small wad of cotton back and forth through the ring. Any scratches or cracks in the ring will catch the cotton fibers and let you know that the guide needs to be replaced. Failure to replace the damaged guide will cause weak points in the line as the line rubs across the rough area.

Guide Repair

Guides are not that difficult to replace. All that is needed is an appropriately sized guide and one of the myriad colors of rod-

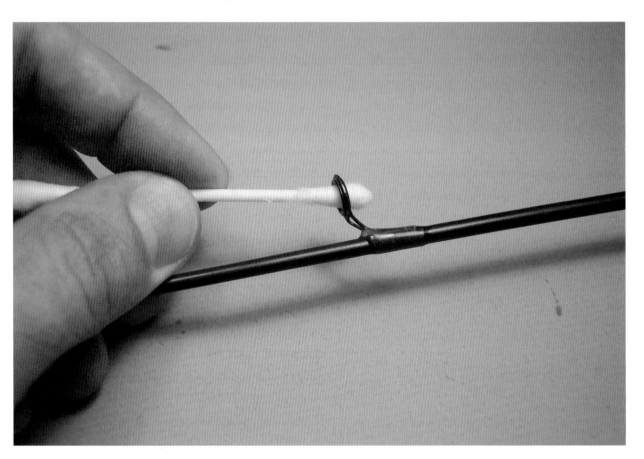

■ Use a cotton swab or small wad of cotton to check guide rings for cracks or nicks. Any roughness or imperfection will catch the cotton fibers, revealing the problem area.

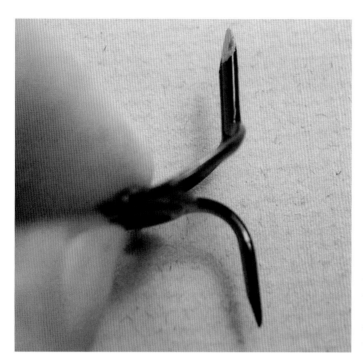

■ To allow the wrapping thread to make a smooth, easy transition from the blank to the guide, the guide foot ends should be filed down to a knifelike edge. Compare the top foot that has been filed to the bottom foot, which has not.

wrapping thread, both readily available from rod-making supply houses. Whether repairing guides that are damaged but still in place or guides that have broken away from the rod blank, the process is the same. The first step is to remove the existing guide, the varnish, and the old wrapping thread.

If the guide has pulled loose from the wrappings, there will likely be an area of broken thread and varnish that is a good starting point for peeling away the remaining material. Use your thumbnail, a table knife, or some other dull edge to catch and hold the material and peel it away from the blank. If the thread won't easily come off the blank, it may be helpful to carefully apply some heat to the varnish to soften it. A forced-air heat gun works well. The idea is to just soften the varnish enough so it can be peeled away from the blank.

If the guide is still in place, take a single-edge razor blade and whittle away the thread and varnish in one area to get a starting point to peel off the rest. You must be very careful when doing this to avoid nicking the blank itself. This can be achieved by cutting with very shallow strokes on top of the guide foot and whittling toward the guide ring. The metal guide foot will prevent the blade from doing damage to the rod blank.

After all the old thread and varnish have been removed and there is only the smooth underlying surface of the blank, it is time to prepare the guide. To get the thread to smoothly transition from the blank onto the guide foot, the foot must be filed down to a sharp edge. This can be done with either a hand file or a small rotary tool grinding stone. The idea is to grind the guide foot so the ends taper out to almost a knifelike edge. After filing or grinding, drag the bottom of the guide foot across a file or stone to remove the burr edge that often forms and can cut into the blank, causing a weak point.

Once this is accomplished, place the guide on the rod blank and check to see if both edges of the guide foot make full contact with the blank. If they do not fully rest on the blank, carefully bend them to get a good fit.

Now it is time to wrap the guide. But first, we need to assemble some simple tools to aid in this task, beginning with something to hold the rod for wrapping. Although many different styles of rod wrappers are commercially available, they are designed and priced with the custom rod builder in mind, not someone who just replaces one or two guides a year. A few minutes searching around the house should come up with a suitable alternative, though. A medium-size heavy cardboard box can be used to hold the rod by cutting a V-shaped notch on two ends of the box. Another idea is to use two wire clothes hangers. Bend the hook of each hanger by 90 degrees, then rotate it 90 degrees. Arrange the two hangers on the edge of your work table so the hooks are hanging just over the edge of the table about 2 feet apart. Secure the hangers with shop clamps, and wrap masking tape around the wire hooks to protect the rod during the wrapping. A third alternative is to spend a few minutes with some lumber scraps and make two simple stands with a shallow

notch at the top. Again, masking tape or something similar should be used in the notches to protect the rod.

The next tool needed is a thread tensioner. Again, there are commercial products available that do a great job, but for our purposes, all you need is probably close at hand. A coffee cup can be used as a thread holder, and a heavy book like a dictionary can be appropriated as your thread tensioner. Place the spool of thread in the cup to keep it from rolling away as thread is pulled off. Open the book in the middle and run the thread across the page from top to bottom. Close the book, and the weight of the pages on top of the thread provides the tension. If more tension is desired, move the thread farther into the pages or place a heavy object on the book. If less tension is needed, place the thread so there are fewer pages on top of it.

Thread tension is important to achieving a good wrap, but there is no hard-and-fast guideline. The idea is for the thread to be very snugly wrapped, but not so tight that the guide can't be moved at all when the wrap is complete. The best idea is to start with what feels right, and when the wrap is complete, if the guide can only be wiggled from side to side with heavy finger pressure, the tension is about right. After time, experience will be your guide to getting the correct thread tension.

The last tool needed is very simple. Cut a piece of heavy thread or braided fishing line. Double it over and securely knot the end so a closed loop is formed. This will be used to pull the tag end of the wrapping thread back under the wrap when the wrapping process is complete, so keep the loop close at hand.

Once the rod is in the holder and the thread has been prepared, place the guide on the blank in the exact same location as the old one. Temporarily secure the guide to the rod by placing a thin strip of tape over the guide foot. The tape should be located as near to the guide ring as possible, since the leading end of the guide foot needs to remain uncovered so thread can be wrapped on it to secure the guide when the tape is removed. When the guide is taped on the rod, try to place it so the guide ring lines up with the other guide rings. Don't worry if it isn't perfect, though. If the guide is wrapped correctly, it can still move freely enough to make some minor adjustments after wrapping and before applying varnish.

To decide where to start the wrap in relation to the guide, simply look at the guide closest to the one being replaced and size your wrap accordingly. Keeping the new wrap the same size as those on either side of it will result in a more aesthetically pleasing end-product.

■ Start a thread wrap by crossing the thread over itself one time while holding the loose end tight against the rod. This takes a little practice to master, but is not that difficult.

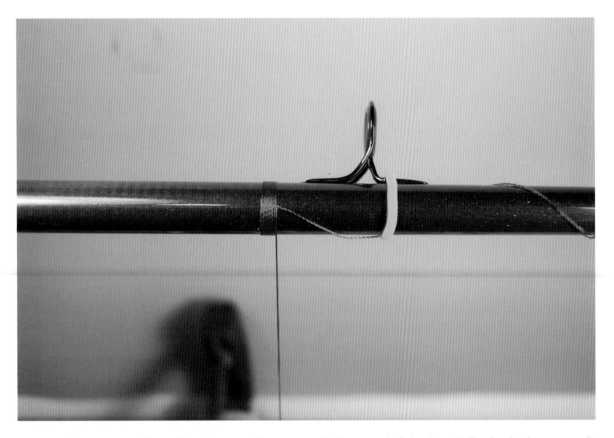

■ Once several turns have been made to secure the loose end of the thread after beginning a wrap, it is time to trim away the loose end and continue the wrap. An orthodontic rubber band is being used here to hold the guide in place; a thin strip of tape also works well.

The next step can be frustrating, but give it a few tries and shortly it will become second nature. Pass the thread over the blank and pull 4 inches or more back toward you. Pinch the loose end of the thread against the blank with your thumb at the desired starting point. Take the loose end and lay it on the rod blank, going toward the guide. Holding the thread where it crosses the blank in place with your thumb and the loose end parallel and tight to the blank, turn the rod to cross the threads by forming an X. Continuing to hold the thread in place, make five or more turns over the loose end, securing the

thread to itself. Trim the loose end flush to the wrap by cutting it with a fresh razor blade. There is a right and wrong way to do this. Position the blade parallel but at a shallow angle to the blank, with the blade edge where the loose end emerges from the wrap. Pull the thread back toward the wrap and against the edge of the blade. If the blade is sharp, it won't be necessary to "saw" the thread against the blade to cut it. A sharp blade will cut clean without fraying, and since the thread was being pulled back against the wrap when it was cut, the cut end should virtually disappear under the wrap.

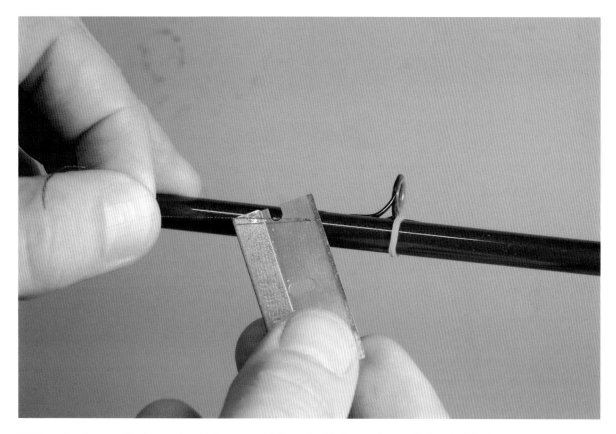

▥ Use a fresh razor blade to trim the loose end. Place the blade nearly parallel to the blank where the loose end protrudes from the wrap and pull the loose end back against the blade instead of "sawing" forward with the blade. Done correctly, the result will be a clean cut without fraying, where the cut end virtually disappears into the wrap. Any small gaps in the wrap can be tightened up by sliding the wraps together with a thumbnail and finished by burnishing to flatten the thread.

Continue to wrap thread up to the guide foot. Once the guide foot is reached, if the edges were properly filed down, the thread will smoothly jump from the blank onto the guide foot. If it doesn't, use your thumbnail to position the wrap and help the thread make a smooth transition.

Keep wrapping the guide to the point where six to eight more wraps will complete the process. Halt here, and while still holding tension on the thread, lay in the loop that was prepared earlier. Position the loop so the knotted end is to the wrap, the looped end to the guide. Leave about an inch of the loop sticking out past where the wrap will end. Complete the last few wraps by wrapping the thread over the looped line. At the end of the last wrap, hold the tension on the wraps by placing your thumb on the thread. Cut the thread several inches away from the rod, then take the loose end of the thread and run it through the loop. Hold the end of the cut thread to maintain tension, and with your other hand holding the knotted end of the loop, use the loop to pull the loose end of the thread back under the last few wraps and out. Trim using a razor blade.

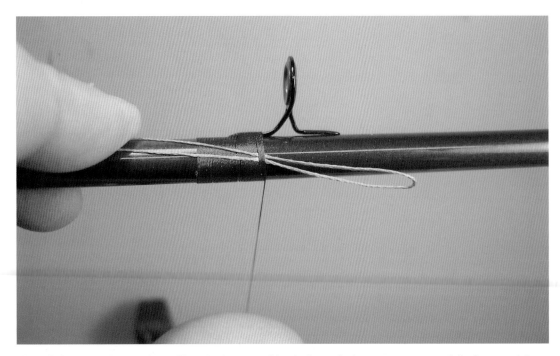

■ To finish a guide wrap by pulling the loose end back through the wrap to secure it before applying the finish, lay in a loop of strong thread or fishing line four to five turns before the end of the wrap. The loop provides a mechanism to pull the loose end back under the wraps while still maintaining tension, thereby locking it in place.

■ Hold the loose end to maintain tension on the wraps, and in one smooth motion pull the loop through the wrap. The loop will pull the loose end from your fingers and carry it with the loop through the wrap to secure the loose end in place.

Once the wrap is complete, the next step is to remove any thread fibers, or "fuzzies," that are sticking out from the wrap. Even a very thin fiber will cause problems when applying the varnish. Using the flame from a lighter, or even better, an alcohol burner, rotate the rod while carefully holding the flame an inch or so from the wrap. The heat from the flame will remove any fuzzies by melting them away.

Check the position of the rod guides to make sure they are all lined up properly. This can be achieved by holding the rod out at arm's length and sighting down it, or by placing it in the holder and looking at it from above to see that the rings are centered on the blank. Make any adjustment to the new guide by carefully wiggling it back and forth into position.

The final step before applying the finish is to burnish the wrap. Burnishing evenly spaces the wrap to fill in any small gaps and flattens the thread for a nice, smooth appearance. The barrel of a ballpoint pen—or any other smooth, rounded surface—is a good tool to burnish the wrap. Rub the tool briskly back and forth across the thread while applying firm pressure.

Now it is time to apply the finish. First, though, there is a decision to be

■ All the glues and finishes needed to make rod repairs.

made based on how you would like the wrap to look. If you want the thread to keep its true color when the varnish is applied, apply a coat of color preserver to the wrap and let it thoroughly dry before applying the varnish. If you prefer a darker, translucent look, dispense with the color preserver and apply the varnish directly to the thread wrappings. By design, color preserver prevents the varnish from penetrating into the threads and to the blank, so the wrap is not quite as strong. From a theoretical standpoint, this may seem to be a drawback, but from a practical standpoint, it will make no difference at all. Either way, if wrapped properly, the guide should stand up to years of use and abuse.

There are many brands of rod finishes available, and all work well. However, each formulation has subtle variations in its working properties and drying time. Two-part epoxies are the standard and are relatively easy to work with. The key to good results is to get the perfect ratio of resin to hardener. If the mix is off, the finish may remain tacky or have other problems. Use a clean set of metal measuring spoons to measure out equal parts of resin and hardener per the manufacturer's instructions. A little finish goes a long way, so it may be tempting to use the smallest measuring spoon possible to save on material. There is a problem with this approach, though. It is absolutely imperative that the finish be mixed in an equal ratio. When using very small amounts, even a few drops difference

between Part A and Part B is going to throw off the 1:1 ratio. By using a larger amount of finish (within reason), some may be wasted, but a few drops difference is proportionally going to have less effect on the required 1:1 ratio.

To mix the finish, lay out a piece of clean aluminum foil on a smooth work surface. Measure out equal parts of the finish and mix thoroughly with a clean Popsicle stick or similar object. While it is very important that the two parts are mixed thoroughly, you want to avoid introducing any more air bubbles into the mixture than absolutely necessary. Once the finish is mixed, let it stand for a few minutes per the manufacturer's directions. During this time, many air bubbles will come out of the solution on their own. One trick to speeding up the process is to closely exhale on the puddle of rod finish. For some reason, this brings the bubbles to the top, where they pop and disappear. Another trick is to heat the mixture. Take a lighter and briefly apply indirect heat underneath the aluminum foil. This will help eliminate any bubbles and also serves to thin the finish.

Apply the finish to the rod wrap with a clean, small craft brush. You may find it easiest to start by lightly dabbing the brush in the finish, then hold the brush against the rod while turning the rod to get a smooth, even edge at either end of the wrap. Apply finish to the remainder of the wrap using long, even strokes running parallel to the rod. Be sure to work finish

■ Most rod finishes and glues are two-part solutions. It is very important that the two parts be mixed in exactly the correct ratio. Mix on a piece of foil using a Popsicle stick. This allows air bubbles introduced during the mixing process to be released.

into the gaps where the guide foot meets the rod. A toothpick works well for this task. Closely examine the finish for any bubbles, and remove them by exhaling on the finish, or if they are large enough, popping the bubbles with a toothpick.

Do not overdo it when applying the finish. If you apply too heavy a coat, sagging can be a problem. It is better to provide one light coat of finish, let it dry, and then apply another light coat instead of trying to do it all in one fell swoop.

Once the finish is applied, it needs to dry for quite some time to fully harden. Drying time is affected by the temperature and humidity of your work area. To prevent sagging during the drying process, the rod must be rotated to keep the finish evenly distributed. Rod makers employ some type of rod drying device that constantly rotates the rod using a small electric motor. However, satisfactory results can be achieved simply by leaving the rod in the holder you used to wrap it and then giving it a partial turn by hand every ten or fifteen minutes for the first two hours of drying, assuming you are working in a warm, low-humidity environment. After two hours, the finish should have set up enough to prevent sagging, but it will remain tacky for several more hours, so avoid touching it until the next day.

After the curing period is over, examine the guide. Any imperfections can be sanded smooth and wiped clean, then another thin coat of finish can be applied to restore the shine to the area that was sanded.

Tip Repair

Replacing a tip is much easier than replacing a guide. If the ring has broken or popped out of the tip, remove the old tip by grasping it with pliers while releasing the glue by applying even, gentle heat to the barrel of the tip with a lighter flame. Purchase a tip in the appropriate ring and barrel size and a stick of rod tip glue (it is a good idea to keep a selection of tips and a stick of glue in your tackle box spares kit since broken rod tips are a common ailment on the water). Lightly roughen the area of the blank where the tip will go with sandpaper to provide a good holding surface for the glue. Apply heat to the end of the glue stick with a lighter and evenly smear some glue on the blank, then quickly place the tip on the blank, making sure to line it up with the other guides. Hold the tip in place a few seconds until the glue hardens, then peel off any excess glue that has collected on the blank.

If the problem is that the rod blank itself has broken near the tip, perhaps all is not lost. The rod could possibly be salvaged by placing a new, larger barrel tip on it. The rod action will likely become slightly heavier, but not to a great extent as long as the break is close to where the original tip was.

Clean the break by cutting the blank just behind any jagged edge or split. Use a thin cutting disk on a rotary tool or a triangular file to get a smooth cut. Select a tip that fits the blank and follow the steps above to glue the tip in place. If you wish, you can add a thread wrap to the tip to dress up the rod.

Other Repairs

Minor gouges in cork rod grips are easily repaired. If the grip is damaged, scrape out any loose material. The hole can be filled with wood putty or a mixture of cork dust and wood glue. Make your own cork dust by using a rasp or rough file on a piece of scrap cork. To collect the dust, file over a piece of aluminum foil and then bend the foil to collect all of the dust in one area. Add some wood glue to the cork dust and mix thoroughly to form a thick paste. Fill in the damaged area with the paste using a Popsicle stick or similar tool. Let dry and sand smooth.

Other repairs that might be needed include loose butt caps. These can be secured in place with waterproof two-part epoxy. Foregrips that have come loose and are twisting on the rod can be secured by using epoxy and a large-gauge hypodermic needle slid in as far as possible, using the gap between the grip and the blank to place the glue where it needs to go. Depending on how the rod was constructed, this technique may also work to secure a loose rear grip. Apply heat to the butt cap with a heat gun to remove it, use the needle to place epoxy deep in any gaps between the grip and the blank, then replace the butt cap.

After performing all of the rod maintenance activities described above, you will have acquired 90 percent of the skills needed to build a custom rod from scratch, which is a very rewarding hobby in itself. If you choose to take the next step and build your own rod, there are many informative books and Web sites available to show you how.

CHAPTER NINE

Maintaining Other Tackle

Maintenance isn't just required on the most complex mechanical tackle, but also on the most basic. As anglers, we should want to get the most from our tackle with a goal of sharp hooks, floating floats, shiny spinner blades, swivels that spin freely, line that is always fresh and strong, and so on.

Line

Perhaps nothing is more important than the condition of our fishing line, since the line is what connects us to the fish. Fishing line has made great strides in the last few decades and is actually pretty amazing stuff when you think about the task it is asked to perform and the stresses put on it.

Fishing line, whether it be monofilament or one of the braided types, is easy to maintain. Store it in a cool, dry place out of the sunlight to prevent ultraviolet breakdown. While fishing, frequently check the last few feet of line for nicks or frays. Cut the damaged portion away, retie the lure or hook, and you are ready to go.

Monofilament line that starts shedding a chalky dust is in need of replacement. Braided lines often lose their coloring and turn almost white over time, especially the first few feet off the spool. This isn't a sign of weak line, but just the dye being worn away from the material. Color can easily be restored, at least for a short time, by running a permanent marker up and down the last few feet of line to help hide it underwater.

Another thing about braided line to keep in mind is that the material is very slick—so slick, in fact, that securing the line to the spool can be a problem. This seems especially true with baitcasting reels. Many reels have been sent in for repair under the assumption that something was wrong with the drag since the reel would play out line under pressure no matter how much the drag was tightened down. What may be happening is the braided line is turning on the spool. Moisture seems to exacerbate the problem, but it can happen at any time.

There is a quick test for this problem. Completely tighten the drag and clamp a thumb down tight on the spooled

🔳 Monofilament line will break down over time. If the line sheds a chalky substance when you run a finger across it, it should be replaced.

line, being careful not to touch the sides of the spool. Now, turn the reel handle with some force. If the handle won't turn, everything is fine—the drag and line on the spool are holding. If the handle does turn, look at the side of the spool while the handle is moving. Do you see the spool moving? Is the line under your thumb moving? If the answer to the first question is yes and the second is no, then the whole collection of line is spinning on the spool.

Although baitcasters are the worst culprits, no matter what type of reel you are spooling with braided line, the corrective

maintenance solution is very easy. Simply put 10 to 15 feet of monofilament backing on the reel, tie the monofilament to the braid, and then finish filling the spool with braid. The monofilament doesn't slip on the spool, so having the actual connection to the spool made with monofilament solves the problem.

For fly-fishing anglers, line maintenance is a more pressing issue. Fly lines get worn in different ways, including mechanical wear and friction from passing through the guide rings, getting stepped on or tangled, dragging over rocks, and so on. Most fly lines are manufactured with a built-in lubricant that helps the line slip through the guides and float high, both of which are important for casting ease and making a good presentation.

To maintain your fly line, rinse it in clean water after each trip. If stored in tight coils, fly line is prone to take a set, a phenomenon known as "line memory." After washing, it's best to store line on a large arbor or spool that allows for big, loose coils and plenty of ventilation to help prevent both line memory and mildew.

Several times a year, take the maintenance a step further by soaking the line in hot, soapy water for an hour or two before cleaning. A very gentle cleanser (such as baby shampoo) is best, as harsh detergents can damage the line's self-lubricating properties. After cleaning, line dressing can be applied sparingly.

Although the fly line backing doesn't require as much attention, it shouldn't totally be ignored or it may not be there when you need it. Backing can have weak spots from being rubbed along the stream bottom or a log during a fight, and it can become clogged with salt residue or dirt and grime to the point where it doesn't come off the spool smoothly when a big fish is taking line. The solution is simple. After the fly line is off the reel, rinse the backing with fresh water and run it through your fingers to feel for rough spots, which will most likely be near where the connection of backing to fly line is made.

Hooks, Lures, and Plugs

Hooks are what directly connect the fish to the angler, so the importance of having a sharp hook cannot be overstated. Sharpness will greatly increase your hookup ratio and also reduce the number of fish that manage to throw the hook. The time for hook maintenance is always. Check the hook before you tie it on, check the hook after every fish is landed, and periodically check the hook even if you aren't catching fish. Dragging over rocks, shell, etc., will quickly dull a hook. Any time a hook won't immediately catch when lightly dragged across a fingernail, give it a few strokes with a hook hone to bring it back to needle sharpness.

Lures and plugs are low maintenance. Constantly check the hooks, but beyond that, periodically look at split rings and hook hangers to determine if they need to be replaced or if the screws need to be tightened. Plug bodies or spinner blades that have become dulled can be brought back to life by scrubbing with some toothpaste, baking soda, or some other mild polishing compound on a wet brush and then rinsing with fresh water. If the finish is badly damaged, touch it up with some epoxy model paint, although lure paint jobs probably do more to attract the fisherman than the fish. Given that more times than not a beat-up, scarred lure will catch just as many fish as an incredibly lifelike one fresh out of the package, lure action must be more important than its paint job.

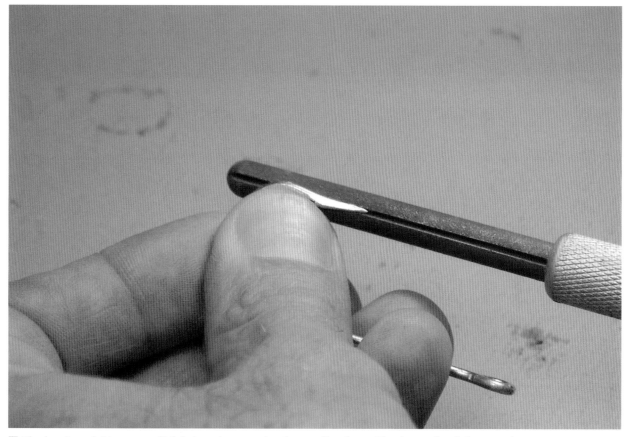

■ The key to catching more fish is keeping your hooks needle-sharp. Check your hook frequently while fishing, and touch up as needed with a hook hone.

As for lures equipped with rubber skirts, the skirts are often held in place with a small rubber collar. Over time the collar can begin to deteriorate, causing the skirt to slip down the hook or else fall apart completely. The quick and easy fix is to supplement the collar with a few wraps of soft, thin wire to hold the skirt in place. Make three or four tight turns around the skirt with the wire, then twist the wire ends together and trim closely with a pair of cutters. The skirt itself will hide the wire, so there's no need to get too pretty here.

Soft plastic lures like rubber worms and grubs are not immune to maintenance.

Got a bag of soft plastics that turned that whitish, faded color from soaking in water trapped in the bag or a tackle box? Empty the bag out on the bed of a pickup, a sidewalk, or other solid surface on a bright and sunny day for a few hours, and the original color will come back just as vibrant as it ever was.

Finally—and this goes for any type of terminal tackle, whether it be hooks, swivels, or whatever—if it gets anywhere close to salt water, rinse it off at the end of each trip! Fail to do so, and you will be sorry. The lures that were actually used need to be rinsed thoroughly, and even a tackle box left open for a few minutes and

■ The collars used to secure rubber skirts on lures eventually fail, causing the skirt to slip down the hook or fall apart completely. A few wraps of soft wire is a quick and easy solution to this problem.

exposed to windblown spray needs a rinsing. Many popular tackle boxes today use interchangeable plastic trays. The benefits are many, but one of the most handy things about the trays is how easy they make cleanup. Open the trays, rinse the contents thoroughly with a stream of fresh water, close and latch the lids, and stand the trays up on end. Most of the water will drain right out, but all the plugs, etc., will stay in their assigned compartments. Tilt

the trays to help the last little bit of water run out, open the tray lids, and let them sit in a sunny, ventilated area until everything is clean, dry, salt free, and ready for the next trip.

When it comes to your tackle, pay attention! Just a few simple maintenance tasks will save big bucks, and when the fish of a lifetime is on the line, you won't have to worry about your tackle failing you in your moment of glory.

CHAPTER TEN

Maintaining Fishing Accessories

Just like a high-society debutante, anglers love to accessorize. No angling outfit is complete without all the little accessories that make a day on the water more comfortable and enjoyable. The principles of maintaining angling accessories are the same as maintaining the necessities—that is, preventive maintenance and catching problems before they become a problem.

"Angling accessories" is a loosely defined term. What one angler considers an essential part of the kit, another might consider an extraneous item. However, there are some items that nearly all anglers possess that need to be kept in good working order.

Tackle boxes have come a long way in recent years. From the basic two-tray tackle box of yesteryear to the modular systems of today, a tackle box performs the simple function of organizing and protecting all your terminal tackle. Tackle storage systems should be kept clean and dry. Once a year or so, empty out all your tackle boxes, wash with water and a mild detergent, rinse with fresh water, let dry, and then replace the tackle in an organized and logical manner. This is also a

great time to examine lures for rusted hooks, loose or broken bills, etc., and to see what items you may be running low on and need restocked. Discard or replace any hooks or other items that are rusty before stowing them in the clean box so the corrosion does not affect other tackle.

Knives and pliers are essential angler tools. After each use, rinse or scrub away any dried blood or slime, wipe dry, and store in a protective sheath. Pliers have moving parts, so occasionally apply a few drops of oil to the hinge to keep them working freely. If your pliers have replaceable cutting blades, when oiling the hinge also loosen the tiny set screws that hold the blades in place and give the threads a drop of oil before snugging them back down. Without maintenance, these screws are prone to corrode and freeze in place, making it next to impossible to remove them to replace the cutting blades. Dull knives are an accident waiting to happen, so keep a keen edge on all blades. A sharp blade completes the job much easier and in a controlled manner. Knife sharpening is an art unto itself, but there are various products on the market that help turn a

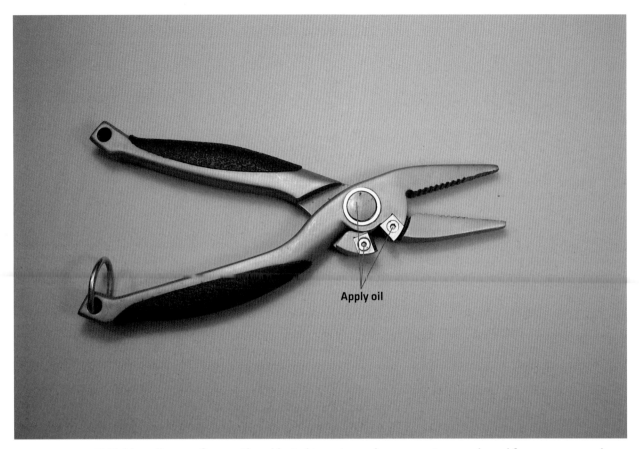

Apply oil

■ Fishing pliers are frequently subjected to water and are prone to corrode and freeze up, so periodically apply a few drops of lubricant to the hinge. For pliers that have replaceable cutting blades, loosen any screws that hold the blades in place and lubricate the threads to prevent the screws from corroding.

skilled job into a simple one that anyone can do.

Gaffs, fish grippers, and spring scales all will benefit from a periodic rinsing with fresh water. Gaff hooks can be touched up with a file to maintain a sharp point that will catch every time. Fish grippers and scales will benefit from periodic light oiling on any pivot points or moving parts.

Landing nets are simple to maintain. Periodically rinse the net with fresh water, check the fasteners for any corrosion and replace as necessary, and examine the net

bag for rips. Net bags can be repaired with nylon twine or plastic cable ties.

Stringers, metal mesh fish baskets, and creels all should be rinsed with fresh water and allowed to dry before storing. Bait wells and buckets should also be washed with fresh water and a mild detergent to remove any slime residue and odor. For really tough cases, add a little bleach to the detergent to remove stubborn odors. After washing, it is important to rinse the items very thoroughly to remove any chemical residue that could be harmful to live bait on the next trip.

Waders, wading boots, and hip boots should all be rinsed with fresh water and hung upside down to dry. Hanging waders and hip boots allows air to circulate to help disperse any trapped moisture and also prevents folds, which will lead to premature failure from dry rot. Small leaks can often be repaired with a wader repair kit, sold at sporting goods stores. If the location of the leak can't be located externally, hook the suspenders or straps to something the correct height off the ground to be fully extended, and slowly and carefully fill them with water to find the leak. Mark the location of the leak with a wax pencil, let the waders dry thoroughly, and make the repair. Another method is the flashlight method. Place a flashlight inside the waders while in the dark. You'll see the light coming through any area with a hole, which can be marked for repair.

A quality rain suit can be an angler's best friend. Always allow your rain suit to dry before stowing it away for the next use. Store it loosely folded in a ventilated area to prevent any mildew or mustiness.

CHAPTER ELEVEN

Tackle Craft

Do you want to be the envy of your fishing buddies? Would you like to have a tackle box stocked with creations that look so good no self-respecting fish could turn them down? Are you having a hard time finding your favorite lure in that particular pattern that always produces like gangbusters but unfortunately is now out of production? Would you like to try a hobby that not only is very enjoyable in itself, but also will lead to catching more fish?

■ A couple of the different types of lures you can make at home. Both jigs and tailspinner-type lures are easily produced given the correct mold and supplies. These lures are awaiting the final steps of attaching skirt material or installing the hook. An airbrush set to give a splatter effect was used to put the highlight color on the top lure.

If the answer to any of these questions is yes, then tackle craft may be for you. Tackle craft is simply making your own fishing tackle, primarily various types of lures. Although not considered maintenance, as it deals with constructing lures from scratch, many of the same principles apply to tackle craft and the same skills are used in both activities. Too, like maintenance, the level you take it to is up to you. Some tackle crafters may start with a block of wood, a handful of hooks and other hardware, and some paint, and end up with a plug that is suitable for either display in a glass case on the mantel or use on the water, hopefully dangling from the mouth of a trophy fish. Other anglers may prefer to construct their lures by purchasing premanufactured components from tackle supply houses and saving some money by assembling the components themselves. Either way you do it, there is great satisfaction in catching fish with a creation of your own hands.

The first thing that comes to many anglers' minds when thinking of constructing their own tackle is fly tying, and with good reason. Fly tying is an art and a science, and the skilled practitioner can pull out a portable fly-tying kit, sit down on a streamside rock, and after a few minutes' work with thread, feathers, and fur, create an incredibly lifelike representation of the insects seen in the stream. Since fly tying is such an art and there are hundreds, if not thousands, of different fly patterns all calling for different materials and techniques to produce the finished product, the subject is far outside the scope of this book. Anglers who have an interest in getting started will find many books and other resources available to help them out.

What anglers may not be as familiar with is crafting other lures, including jigs, weights, spinners, plastic worms, and plugs. The techniques used to produce these pieces of tackle range from extremely basic to moderately skilled but are skills anyone can learn and put into practice in just a few minutes.

Jigs and Weights

Most jigs and weights are constructed using molten lead and a mold. Lead is heated to a liquid form and poured into a mold where, as it cools and solidifies, it takes the shape of the mold cavity. The end result is a piece of tackle that can be used as is or painted to make it even more attractive.

When working with lead, safety is first and foremost. Lead is a poisonous metal that can damage nervous connections and cause blood and brain disorders. Long-term exposure to lead has very serious implications, so all the proper precautions should be followed, including wearing protective gear to prevent lead coming in contact with bare skin and working in a well-ventilated area to minimize exposure to fumes.

Pure lead melts at 621.5 degrees Fahrenheit. The low melting point, along with

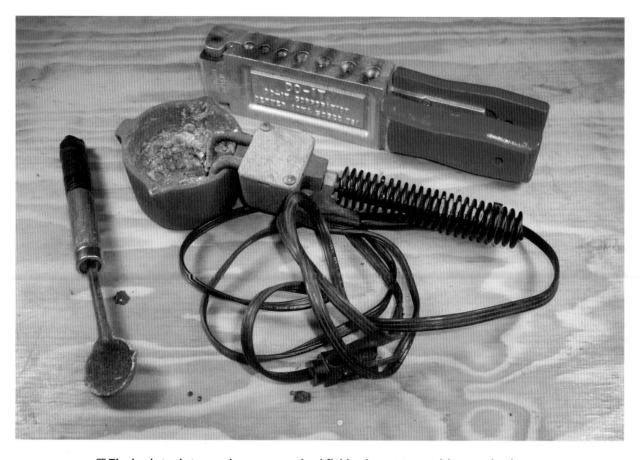

■ The basic tools to pouring your own lead fishing lures are a melting pot, lead ladle, and lure mold.

its malleability and density, makes it an ideal substance for manufacturing certain types of fishing lures. While the melting point may be low relative to other metals, it certainly does not feel low when the lead comes in contact with bare skin. Molten lead can cause very serious burns. Again, protective gear is a must as are safe handling practices. The number one thing to keep in mind is that molten lead and water do not mix. Water or moisture introduced into a pot of molten lead can lead to disastrous results, as the lead can explode violently and splatter anything in its path.

Lead has been used in tackle craft for many years, however, and as long as a few commonsense rules are always followed, the process is an easy and safe one. The rules to keep in mind are:

1. Always use protective gear and a ventilation system that pulls fumes away from the work area.
2. Don't eat, drink, or smoke while working with lead, and don't have anything of that nature in your work area that could result in lead being ingested.
3. Never allow children around the work area, and only work with lead when you

can devote your full attention to the task at hand.

4. Ensure you have a safe and sturdy work area to hold your supply and an adequate device designed for melting and pouring lead.

5. Make sure no moisture or water is present either in the material itself or near the work area.

The sources of lead are many, but all lead is not equal for pouring lures. The purer the lead, the easier it melts and pours. Pure lead is also soft, though, with the drawback that a lure made of soft lead can be dented by a hard bump against a rock, which usually results in the paint chipping off. On the other hand, since pure lead flows easier, it is better for pouring small molds that have small cavities. Good-quality lead can be purchased in small ingots from tackle craft and reloading supply houses, but a little searching around your community should turn up enough material at little or no cost to keep you busy pouring lures for a long time.

Old tire weights are one of the easiest sources to find, but tire weights are not pure lead; instead, they are a lead alloy with antimony and tin mixed in with the lead. This alloy melts at a higher temperature but is harder than lead alone, so denting is less of a problem. However, alloy doesn't poor as smoothly, so completely filling small cavities is more of a problem. In addition, tire weights are often coated with road grime and oil and are equipped with a steel clip. These problems aren't huge, but it does mean you will spend more time ladling impurities off the top of the pot of molten lead.

Scrap yards may also be a good source of lead, though the material will likely be an alloy of some type. Lead pipes were once commonly used in residential water systems, and a few short pieces will result in many fishing lures. Along those lines, plumbing supply houses may still have some lead on hand, since it was once commonly used to seal joints on soil lines. Old batteries may seem to be a good choice, but they are not. Never use old batteries for lead!

One source of excellent-quality, clean lead that you may not think of is your local dentist's office. The little piece you bite down on when you get an X-ray during your checkup actually has a thin layer of lead foil inside. It takes a lot of pieces of foil to make a lure, but if you can talk the dental office into saving it for you, a busy practice can supply more than enough lead to meet your lure-making needs.

The steps to pouring lead are simple. Heat the lead to a good working temperature, and while that is taking place, prep the mold. Molds give better results the first few pours when they have been prepped. The first step is to hold the mold open over a candle until the black soot from the flame completely coats the cavity. This helps the lead flow more easily into the cavity and also gives the pieces a nice, smooth finish. The next step is to

are available. But, if you prefer to save a little money or wish to make your own custom creations (which is really the fun of tackle craft), you can buy skirt material in a myriad of colors that you can combine, with a little of this and a little of that, to get exactly what you envisioned. Skirt material comes in solid pieces, so each individual strand does not have to be held in place while securing it to the lure. *Skirt layers* are precut and solid on either one or both ends, so they are easy to work with—when you are done and ready for the skirt to be individual strands, you simply trim off the solid ends to release them.

Multistrand rubber skirt material looks like a ribbon; it's about an inch wide and has the feel of a wide rubber band. What makes up the solid ribbon, though, is forty or more individual strands. When the ribbon is secured to the lure and stretched tight away from the lure, a sharp pair of scissors is used to slowly cut across the end of the ribbon, causing each strand to come loose and become an individual piece.

Skirt material is commonly secured to the lure either by using a skirt collar

◪ Silicone skirt layers come in many colors and glitter patterns. The layers come as one long piece; you simply cut through the solid portion to release an individual layer from the roll. The layer is secured in place, then the solid ends trimmed off to release the filaments.

or wrapping with wire. Skirt collars can be thought of as extremely tight rubber bands. A special tool is used to stretch open the collar, the skirt material is passed through it, and then the hook is threaded through the collar and onto the skirt-keeper part of the lure. Tension is released off the tool, and the collar shrinks back down and holds the skirt in place. Collars have the advantage of being a quick and easy method, but the disadvantage is that they break down over time, which can cause the skirt to constantly slip down onto the hook, or they can break off completely, allowing the skirt to fall apart and be lost.

The more time-consuming but more durable method is to hold the skirt in place with a few wraps of thin wire. This can take a little bit of practice to get the hang of, but gives good results. The skirt is held in place on the lure and then, leaving several inches of wire at the beginning point, two or three tight wraps of wire are made around the lure. A twist is made by crossing the wire left at the beginning point with the coil of wire that remains. Done properly, one or two twists are all

■ This skirt collar is failing. A close look reveals the collar material has deteriorated and needs to be replaced with a new collar or wrapped with wire.

that is needed, and then the two ends of the wire can be worked back and forth to break off right at the twist. If it doesn't work out quite this way, don't sweat it—just take a pair of wire cutters and trim the wire as close to the twist as possible. It will be hidden under the skirt, and the fish aren't going to be judging your wire twisting abilities anyway. You should now have a finished lure that is ready for the water.

Soft Plastic Lures

Lures made of soft plastic, like rubber worms and grubs, can be crafted at home too. Given the reasonable price of these lures and the fantastic color selection available commercially, one might wonder, why mess with making your own? There could be several reasons. Hand-poured plastic worms have a subtle action that is different than the mass-produced, injection-molded soft plastics. Also, making your own worms allows you to fine-tune how soft or hard (stiff) the worm will be, which not only influences how the lure works through the water, but also its durability. Finally, frugal anglers will be glad to know that soft plastic baits are completely recyclable. Got a plastic worm that has caught a few fish but the head is torn to where it won't stay up on the hook anymore? Save it, melt it down, and use it to make a new worm.

As with the melting of lead, safety is foremost when working with molten plastic. Worm plastic melts at about 350

degrees Fahrenheit—plenty hot to cause a painful burn. Adding to this danger is the fact that hot plastic sticks to anything it touches. Splatter some on the back of your hand, and it's there until you peel it off. A quick flick of the wrist isn't going to get the hot substance off you, instead it sticks and burns. Thin gloves, a long-sleeved shirt, and safety glasses will take care of any splatters, though.

Plastic gives off fumes as it is melted, especially if it gets too hot and the plastic begins to scorch. While plastic fumes aren't as dangerous as lead fumes, the unique smell isn't something the rest of your household will likely enjoy, so be sure to work in a well-ventilated area or even outside in a garage or workshop.

Pouring plastic takes just a few supplies, and the first is a mold. Molds come in flexible rubber or hard plastic and in various configurations, or you can make your own. Keep in mind that hand-poured plastics are not completely round like injection-molded plastics. One side of the lure will be somewhat flat. While this may not be as aesthetically pleasing to the eye, you can trust that the fish won't care a bit.

To make your own mold, find a worm design that is close to what you want. If you like the head section of one design and the tail section of another, cut each worm in half and then join the halves by slightly melting the ends over a flame and holding them together until the plastic cools and bonds the two pieces. Next, mix some plaster of paris and pour it into a shallow container. Take the worm and press it down into the plaster of paris to where the worm is flush with the surface. Let the plaster cure until hard, pull out the worm, scrape away any lumps or ridges, and give the mold several coats of enamel spray paint. The spray paint helps fill in the rough plaster to give the finished worm a smooth, shiny finish. Now you have a mold that is ready to birth hundreds, if not thousands, of plastic worms.

Plastic liquid is the primary material used to make soft plastic lures. The material is a thin, white liquid that when heated, changes to a soft, clear plastic. The desired color is achieved by adding drops of coloring, and the properties of the plastic may be adjusted by mixing in softener or hardener. Other substances like glitter and scents may also be added to the mix.

A cheap aluminum saucepan with a pouring spout (if it doesn't have one, just make one by bending the lip of the pan with a pair of pliers), a stirring spoon, and a heat source are all you need. Your kitchen stove will work just fine for the job of heating the plastic, but don't forget the caution about making your house smell like a chemical plant! A better idea is to pick up an old electric hot plate at a flea market or garage sale. The hot plate is compact and portable, and if you spill some plastic on it, who cares?

The first step is to lay out your molds and heat the plastic. If recycling old plastic lures, just throw a few in the pan on moderate heat and stir occasionally as the plastic melts. If you are using plastic liquid, pour the desired amount into the pan and heat until the material turns clear and thickens to the consistency of heavy syrup. Stir in the desired colors, and you are ready to pour. Hardener works best when it is added to the plastic before heating, while softener should be added after the material is hot.

Pick up the pan and slowly pour the plastic into the mold, starting at one end and moving the length of the mold as it fills. If a multicolor lure is desired, you'll need two pans—one for each color. Pour with the first color to the desired transition point, then immediately continue with the other color so the plastics will bond as they cool. If you want a layered look, do the same thing—fill the mold half full with the first color, then immediately fill the rest of the mold with the other.

Give the plastic a few minutes to solidify and cool, and then carefully pull your new creation out of the mold and start on the next one. Multicavity molds will greatly speed up how many lures you can create at a time, since less time will be spent waiting for each and every worm to cool enough that it doesn't deform when it is removed from the mold.

Plugs

Constructing plugs takes some skill; only the basics will be discussed here. Anglers can simplify the process by purchasing premanufactured bodies, which are available in various designs and come with hook hangers already installed. All the angler has to do is install the hooks and split rings. Premanufactured plug bodies can be purchased finished or unfinished. Unfinished plugs allow you to use the paint scheme of your choice, a step that should be completed before installing the hooks.

If it has always been a dream of yours to catch a fish on a wooden plug that you crafted or whittled yourself, then more work will be required. The first step is to start with a block of wood bigger than the desired final product. Various types of woods can be used, but balsa is a favorite for its light weight and ease of working it into the final shape. Work the lure gradually into shape by taking off larger pieces at first and then slowly working down to the fine details. Rough work can be done with a saw, lathe, rotary tool, rasp, coarse sanding wheel, etc., and then as the lure takes shape, progressively step down to whittling by hand or using detail-work rotary tool attachments. Complete this step by fine sanding to a silky finish.

If the lure has a bill or diving lip, a slot must be cut and the plastic or metal bill installed by gluing it in place with epoxy. This is a crucial step and one prone to failure—get it wrong and the lure won't run right, but you won't know that until much of the building process is complete. However, getting it right can also pay huge dividends.

A fishing buddy of mine broke the bill on a mass-produced minnow-shaped bass plug. Since he had always been fond of that particular lure, he decided to try to save it by replacing the bill, a task he performed by cutting out a piece of hard plastic from a cassette tape case and gluing it into place. After field testing and doing a little fine-tuning by trimming and scraping the sides of the bill with a sharp knife, he ended up with a lure that had a very unique action and, boy, did it catch fish! But, all good things come to an end, and after many years of use, a big fish finally claimed the lure as its own. Replacement lures were bought of the same make and model, and although they caught fish too, none could achieve the fish-catching ability and magic rolling and bobbing action of the repaired one. So, when it comes to designing and handcrafting plugs, it's trial and error. For every success story, there will be many flat-out failures or results that fall somewhat short of what was hoped for.

Once the plug has been crafted and the bill attached, it's time for painting. Painting all types of lures, including plugs, is covered later in this chapter.

After painting, all that is left is to attach the hardware to get a fully functional plug. Small pilot holes are drilled, and threaded hook hangers and a line attachment point are screwed in place. Hooks should be of the appropriate size; often just stepping up or down a size can influence the lure's action in the water.

Some heavy-duty plugs are constructed with a through-wire design where a piece of wire is actually inserted through small holes drilled in the plug to connect the hook hangers and the line tie for greater strength. If this is the case, this step should be performed before painting.

Although we have covered a variety of fishing lures that can be made at home, it is not an exhaustive list. Inline spinners, spoons, offshore trolling lures—all can be made at home. Fact is, if you can buy it, you can probably make a pretty good version of it at home given the proper tools, supplies, time, and skill.

Painting

Lure painting is a subject in and of itself. Savvy anglers are discovering that to get the edge on the competition, sometimes you have to take matters into your own hands. There are several ways to paint lures, but one of the easiest is with an airbrush.

So why paint your own when the quality of mass-produced lures has continued to improve over the years? Today's creations can look so lifelike, it sometimes is hard to tell what is real and what is not.

The fishing lure business is a numbers game, like any business. Sell more lures, make more money. To sell enough lures to recoup the design and tooling costs of bringing a lure to the mass-production line means the finished product must have widespread appeal. Manufacturers can't afford to produce lures that may have limited interest. While this strategy is necessary from a business point of view, it is not the best strategy for anglers. Consider the following.

A few large retailers have cornered the lion's share of the fishing tackle market. While mass merchandising is great for keeping prices low, it puts you, the angler, at the mercy of the buyers for the large retailers. They decide what goes on the shelves or in the catalogs, not somebody who has hands-on experience on your local waters. Who do you think has a better feel for what will work best at your local fishing hole, a corporate buyer or the local angler?

In addition, fishing "used water" is a fact of life nowadays. Do you ever get the feeling that the fish you are casting to could describe every lure by item number and price? The old adage about "fish something different" has truth to it. Tie on a lure the fish haven't seen before, and your chances for success increase.

Finally, there is nothing like the satisfaction of fooling a wise old fish with one of your own creations. While building fishing lures from scratch can be quite an involved process, giving one a spiffy paint job is a snap. Airbrushing has its own tricks of the trade, but even a first-timer can produce respectable results.

So, exactly what is an airbrush, and what business does it have being a part of your fishing gear arsenal? Airbrushing is

■ **A basic airbrush setup and several different types of paint can be used to paint lures.**

simply a method of applying paint. Other lure-painting methods include dipping and brushing, but for creating intricate patterns, neither offers the control and level of detail provided by the airbrush. An airbrush uses compressed air to force paint through a nozzle, thus breaking up the paint into fine droplets.

If you are in the market for an airbrush, there are a few things to keep in mind. Airbrushes range in price from very affordable to pricier professional units. An airbrush that will serve you well for many years shouldn't set you back any more than the cost of a decent fishing reel and, just like a good reel, should last a long time if properly maintained.

Airbrushes come in two basic varieties: single-action and double-action. Think of a single-action unit as a can of spray paint. You configure the spray pattern, and then simply depress the trigger to start spraying. The unit is either on or off. Single-action units are best for uniform application of a single color on a large surface. For just a few dollars more, however, a double-action brush is the choice of most individuals since it provides much greater control. With a double-action airbrush, the trigger controls both the air flow and the paint flow. This means you control how much paint goes through the nozzle at any given time. Pushing down on the trigger controls the air; pulling back on the trigger controls the paint flow. With a little practice, tasks like drawing heavy versus light lines or "feathering" edges will become second nature.

Airbrushes have few working parts, including the tip and needle. Tips and needles are inexpensive and come in several different sizes. Which size is best depends on the viscosity of the material being applied. A #3 tip and needle is probably a good starting point, but it's a good idea to buy a set of different sizes to find out what works best for different types of paint.

Once you have your airbrush, you need something to supply the air that powers the brush. If you have an air compressor in your garage, you already have this base covered. Be sure your compressor has a moisture trap and a way to regulate the air delivery pressure. If not, both items are commonly available anywhere that sells pneumatic tools and accessories. If you don't already have the basic shop air compressor, there are a couple other options. Some small air compressors are specifically designed for airbrush use, and compressed air can also be purchased in disposable cans. Over time, an air compressor is much more economical than the disposable cans.

Now that we have covered the basics of what an airbrush is and how it works, we arrive at what we are going to put through the brush. Different types of paint can be used on lures, and everybody has a favorite. Epoxies, vinyls, and acrylics are all good choices. Each comes in a myriad of colors and has advantages and disadvantages. The Createx line of acrylics is especially popular, though, and two-part epoxies have a strong following too.

When selecting a type of paint, keep cleanup in mind. It is very important to thoroughly clean your airbrush each time you use it. Get lazy about this task, and you will suffer the consequences of poor performance and shortened life of the airbrush. A paint that cleans up with hot, soapy water is a lot easier to deal with than one requiring strong solvents to remove every particle of paint from the brush.

Maybe your artistic talents leave a little to be desired, and you doubt your ability to create something that even the most nondiscriminating fish would find desirable? Don't despair. Painting lures doesn't have to be all freehand work with only a sharp eye and steady hand to guide you. The best results are usually obtained with stencils and masks, and your ingenuity is the only limit to what you can create with these tools. Want a fish-scale look to your lure? Wrap the lure in fine netting before spraying. How about a vertical bar pattern? Take a comb, and hold it up against the lure's body as you spray across it. Where there is a gap between the comb's teeth, the paint will make it onto the lure; where there are teeth, it won't. The closer you hold the comb to the surface being painted, the sharper the edges of the pattern will be; the farther away, the more diffuse the edges.

Reusable stencils can be made with some thin cardboard or a flimsy tin plate. Draw out the pattern you desire (the venerable "coachdog," for example), cut out the openings with a razor knife, and you have a stencil that will produce the same pattern again and again. Remember, hold it close for sharp edges, farther away for fuzzy edges.

Don't want the pattern on the lure's head, just the main body? Use tape to "mask" the part you don't want painted. Whatever you use for a mask, be careful it doesn't stick so well that the underlying paint comes off along with the tape. Using low-tack drafting tape is a good way to avoid this common problem.

If you want to add another level to your fishing, try airbrushing. The ideas mentioned here are just the beginning of how to put your ingenuity and airbrush to work for you to create lures that both fish and fishermen will find eye-catching and almost impossible to ignore.

While most types of lure paint come in liquid form and can be applied by a variety of methods, there is another type to consider. Powder paint lure finish is a great choice for jig heads, spoons, spinner blades, and other compact metal items.

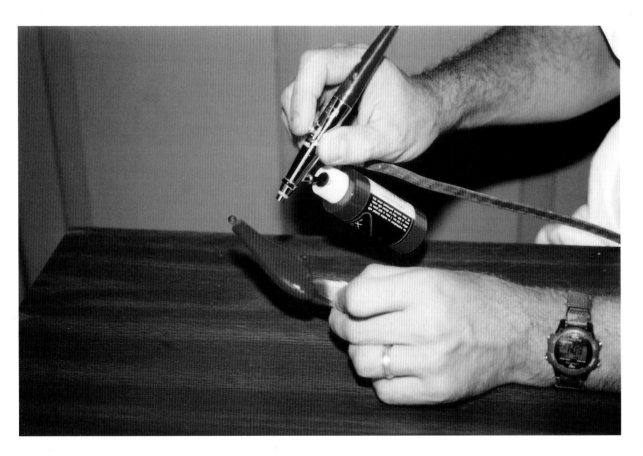

▥ Applying the first coat of paint to a plug. Masking tape can be used to protect the bill or any other area of the plug that you want to remain paint free.

The paint comes in the form of a fine powder. The item to be painted is heated up to the desired temperature over a clean, nonsmoking flame—an alcohol burner or candle with the wick trimmed close works well. While the item is still hot, it is placed in the powder, and upon removal, a hard, glossy finish forms in brilliant color.

Although the process is very easy, technique is important, but with a little practice you will get excellent results. First, make sure to stir the powder until it is fluffy and light. Getting the correct heat is part of the technique, but a rule of thumb is two seconds for 1/16-ounce jigs, four seconds for 1/4-ounce jigs, etc. While hot, quickly swish the jig through the powder with a side-to-side motion to cover the entire surface—do not dip or push the jig into the powder—and remove immediately. The surface will then melt and gloss over. If the jig smokes, reduce the preheat time slightly. If the jig appears powdery and rough, increase the preheat time. Continue to keep the powder stirred as you paint to keep it loose and fluffy.

■ The idea is to swipe the item through loose powder, not push it into packed powder. Powder painting is easy, but your technique is important.

The final step is curing the paint, which will produce an extremely durable, chip-resistant finish. Painted items can be cured by hanging them in an oven set to 350 degrees for fifteen minutes. Always open the eye of the hook with a sharp object before curing; if you forget, you may never get it open!

This chapter is intended to simply provide an introduction to crafting your own fishing tackle. If you decide you would like to pursue tackle crafting in earnest, there are many books and Web sites available to help you improve your skills and fill up your tackle box with homemade—and successful—creations.

CHAPTER TWELVE

A Diamond in the Rough— Finding and Restoring Vintage Tackle

Modern tackle is highly advanced. Manufacturers make full use of high-tech materials, and new and innovative engineering has solved many of the problems anglers once faced. However, new is not always better. Many anglers retain a strong nostalgia for classic fishing tackle for a variety of reasons.

While it is rare for fishing tackle to appreciate in value, some items do. A few are valuable for their uniqueness or rarity. These items fall in the "collectibles" category. The hobby of collecting vintage fishing tackle is a subject in and of itself, and consequently is far outside the scope of this book.

However, some tackle items, especially reels, are simply classics that have stood the test of time and are still in demand by today's angler. For example, the original Zebco Cardinal spinning reels have been off the market for many years but still bring a premium price at online auctions. A reel that sold for less than $20 in its day can now sell for over $100 in mint condition. Many people believe there was no better spinning reel ever made, and they are still actively sought either to add to the angler's arsenal or to keep as a backup for an old favorite.

Another example would be the early Lew Childre baitcasting reels. Again, even though the brand has been sold and resold, and reels are still produced under the Lew's name, the original Lew's reels are still held in high regard by many freshwater bass anglers.

These are just a couple examples from a long list of reel models that anglers have decided are timeless classics and consequently are still in demand.

Why Buy Used?

Vintage reels just can't be beat for quality of components and construction. Like many products, reels in the pre–"disposable society" era were built to last. Buyers back then made an investment in a product and

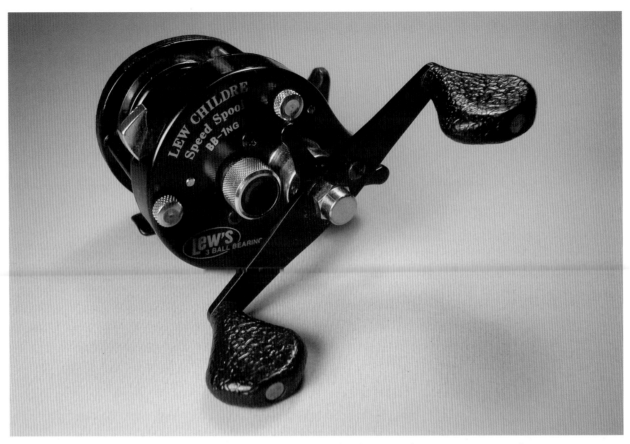

■ Some vintage reels are still highly sought after by anglers and bring top prices on Internet auction sites.

expected it to last a long time, in contrast to buying a product with the understanding it would be put into service for just a few years and then thrown away and replaced with the latest, greatest thing. As with anything, however, there are trade-offs with this approach. When anglers began to demand lightweight high-performance reels, the way to achieve that goal was to build the reels with lighter materials and reduce the number of parts—mechanical functions that were performed by two heavier springs were now performed by one lighter spring, and so on. The result is a reel that feels light in the hand even at

the end of the day, but is perhaps not quite as durable as the old reels were.

Some vintage reels carry a nostalgia value or simply are as comfortable as an old shoe. After years of equipping themselves with the latest thing, some anglers reach a point where they prefer the nostalgia of using old tackle that brings to mind their earlier days. Maybe it was that first bait-casting reel that came one Christmas Day all those years ago and was later traded off to a buddy and replaced with the new-est model. As the years go by, the angler begins to wish the reel was still around for old times' sake and searches for an exact replacement. Or perhaps that same reel has served faithfully for many years, and since its idiosyncrasies are known and accepted and it carries so many memories, when it is lost or broken beyond repair, the desire is to replace it with an exact match to keep the tradition alive.

Along those same lines, occasionally a reel comes on the market with some new design feature or characteristic that never caught on with most anglers, and it is soon discontinued. Some anglers loved that feature, though, and are disappointed to find that modern reels lack it. The solution is to find another reel like it on the vintage market.

Finally, there is often simply money to be saved by buying used. For the most part, fishing tackle does not "wear out." Rods don't wear out, lures don't wear out, reels don't wear out, etc. Rather, rods may need a guide replaced, lures may need a new set of hooks, or reels may need a cleaning and service. In fact, "worn out" is usually synonymous with "needs maintenance." There are some great deals to be had on quality fishing tackle at a bargain price if you are just willing to invest the little time needed to do the maintenance to bring the item back from the dead. Most likely, the cost of the item plus the parts to fix it is still going to be a fraction of what it would cost to buy a brand-new item of similar quality. Over time you will develop a feel for what is worth fixing and what isn't, and what has true value and what doesn't. Nothing is more satisfying,

though, than dropping a $5 bill on a flea market diamond in the rough that "doesn't work right" and a few weeks later is on the water performing like a champ or drawing bids on an auction site.

Finding Vintage Tackle

Places to find vintage tackle include flea markets, yard sales, estate auctions, and, to a lesser extent, online auction sites. Flea markets offer the best selection, but there are some things to watch for. A flea market vendor that specializes in fishing tackle knows exactly what's being sold and what it is worth, so true "finds" are going to be rare. However, flea market prices are always negotiable, so use your knowledge of maintenance to point out potential problems with the item to negotiate a reduced price. Often there will be vendors at flea markets selling a hodgepodge of items that were picked up from yard sales. These vendors are most interested in moving goods, and the items are priced accordingly. This is a case of "the early bird gets the worm." Show up late and any diamonds are long gone, either to another individual on the hunt or to a dealer making the rounds.

Yard sales and estate auctions offer more promise. The seller's main motivation is to clean up and get rid of stuff, no matter what it brings, so just about anything might be for sale. The tackle selection may range from nothing to Uncle

Bob's old fishing gear that has been gathering dust in the garage for years—you won't know until you look. Uncle Bob may have been a casual angler with a few cheap spin-casting outfits, or he may have been a seriously equipped bass angler back in his day. Sellers generally don't really care—they just want the stuff out of their garage. Again, get there early for the best hunting, and remember that although prices are low to begin with, they are still likely to be very negotiable.

That leaves online auction sites. Finding a true steal this way is almost impossible. There are thousands of people on the same search, and the auction nature of the sale means the item will likely go for what it is worth. However, that is not to say auction sites are not highly valuable. For one thing, they are an outlet for reels you have reclaimed and want to sell—this is how you turn yard sale pennies into dollars.

When it comes to finding a particular reel or determining the value of a vintage reel, the auction sites can't be beat. Have a favorite reel that is long out of production and wish you had bought several when they were still on the market? You should be able to find it on an auction site. Have a box full of old reels you picked up at an estate sale and wonder which ones are worth fixing? Search an auction site for complete listings of that model reel to determine what the market says it is worth.

Restoring Vintage Tackle

Once you find your diamond in the rough, getting it back to good working order is not difficult. The steps involved in restoring tackle are the same as they are in maintaining tackle. Take it apart if necessary, thoroughly clean it, replace any bad parts, and reassemble with lubrication as needed. All of this has already been covered, so it does not bear repeating. What does bear repeating, however, are the wonders a little maintenance can do.

I once "caught" a nice baitcasting outfit that some unfortunate soul had lost over the side of a boat. When the rod and reel first came out of the water, dangling from the diving plug that had snagged it, the reel handle would not turn and it was impossible to even determine the make and model. A few hours of work, though, and both the rod and reel were back to full working condition. Once the dirt was gone, what lay underneath was a high-end graphite rod from a top manufacturer and a quality baitcasting reel. Both are still in use today. There was absolutely nothing wrong with either, other than an extremely bad case of the dirties from lying on the bottom of a lake for who knows how long. Cosmetically, the outfit doesn't gleam like it just came off the showroom floor, but functionally, the rod and reel perform just as good as the day they were sold—truly a diamond-in-the-rough find.

■ Heath Pack of Morganton, Georgia, with Blue Ridge Lake smallmouth

■ Cody Marchant (left) and Steve Marchant (right) of Lafayette, Georgia, display a nice redfish caught on Mobile Bay's famous Dixie Bar.

Conclusion

The best anglers are all-around anglers. Great anglers not only understand how to find and catch different species of fish from various habitats in all four seasons, but also can use their tackle like it was an extension of themselves. Before this can be achieved, you have to understand how tackle works, and the best way to reach that level of knowledge is to get familiar with your equipment by maintaining it. Maintaining your tackle will not only provide insight into how best to utilize it, but it will also provide peace of mind. Time on the water spent trying to figure out why your reel doesn't perform as it should—or even worse, time spent trying to fix a problem that could have easily been avoided—is time not devoted to finding and catching fish.

Keep in mind the three types of maintenance. Breakdown maintenance is to be avoided. It will only result in lost time, frustration, and disappointment. The time to find out you have a problem is well before it becomes a problem.

Preventive maintenance is what anglers should strive for. Extend your hobby and invest some maintenance time, using the information in this book to become that all-around angler who truly understands and maintains his or her tackle. The result will be years of trouble-free performance and more enjoyable angling.

The final step is corrective maintenance. Devote some time to thinking about how you can improve your tackle in little ways that will not only increase its service life, but also lead to more enjoyable fishing.

Avoid the first type and utilize the last two types of maintenance to keep your tackle in top form, and you will gain satisfaction not only in a job well done, but also in more productive time on the water.